Tube Cash

"How to Make Extra Cash or Earn a Full Time Living from YouTube"

Written By

Tony Richie

Dedication

I dedicate this book to my wife E and two beautiful daughters, Star and Jo, for believing in me and keeping me strong and motivated during the uncertain and hard times. Although I always had faith and knew that I would make it and do well for us, at times, I did beat myself up inside of my own mind. Sometimes I believe we could all use the strength and inspiration of others to help us get through and back up again. Be it your family, your closest supporters, your God, or your inner self, we all need to talk to somebody at times.

I also dedicate this book to my mother for all of the unconditional love that she gave me, even though I wasn't the best-behaved kid on the block. I thank her for pushing to survive through stage four ovarian cancer with only a thirteen percent chance to survive when I was twelve. I know she fought as hard as she could because she worried about my future coming from a broken family.

To both of my half-brothers. Brother John for taking me in when I was sixteen and needed guidance in life. Teaching me discipline and the basics about money and savings. To my brother, Joe, who also inspired me to keep striving and turning me on to the book that helped me change my mindset "Think and Grow Rich" by Napoleon Hill, when I was in my early twenties.

To my father, Joe. Although you were a true player for life and at times when I was five, six, or seven and never understood why we were hanging out with other women, you always cared for me. For giving me the chance to work with you in the automotive shop to learn about cars and teaching me to make money with my hands. All of this was a stepping stone for me to get to the next level. Thank you, pops.

I also dedicate this book to you, the reader, my future fan (I hope so). I want to thank you for making it a number one, and I also congratulate you for wanting to know more. It shows that you, too, want to better yourself and want to make something of yourself. To be somebody.

Preface

I want to say that, yes, my story may seem crazy and you may think, "well yeah... Tony, you had a skill that you could backpack off of to create something..." I want to say that this is totally BS. You also have something that you can work with. You need to take inventory of yourself right now and work with what you have.

I could have easily made excuses at every level if I wanted to. The going is never easy. If it was easy everybody would be millionaires. Stop making excuses, put your life on a sheet of paper and see what you have to work with and start at where you are, right now.

This book is the real thing. It's my true and solid story of how I literally started with nothing but an idea and a ninety-nine-dollar video camera. I then went on to make millions of dollars online by understanding and using the power of online systems and marketing, and especially how I did it with simple YouTube videos. The best part is, this unfair advantage is available to you right now, and if you're brave enough to believe and act upon the ideas and strategies that I'm about to share with you through this book, your wildest dreams just may come true. Just be careful of what you ask for.

Yes, I could have made this book longer, but the purpose of this book wasn't for me to share every little detail about my life like a biography would, but more to share a quick background of who I am, where I come from, how it all started, and what I was able to do with YouTube and digital marketing so you can get a clear idea and do the same if you think you can. Keyword (think you can). Just like one of my favorite authors, Napoleon Hill, says; "If you believe and think you can, you can."

This is not an end game book. This is the beginning. If you really want success in life, it's yours! It's not rocket science. If you really want to live the good life, have an online business that's running for you 24/7, work from home or anywhere in the world, then get to work because it's all yours.

I wrote this book to inspire and help you open your eyes of what's possible right now in today's digital world. Be careful, it's changing fast. But it's a fact; there are more millionaires created today than there were at any other time in history.

Technology is where it is, but you don't need to be a tech innovator or coder to make a lot of money. You can just learn how to use the systems and leverage it 100X! Yes, the guys who invented YouTube made out like fat rats to the tune of billions. But there are many others, average people like you and I who are carving out their slice of niche audiences and making big money by using the YouTube platform. They didn't invent it, they learned how to use it. The problem is, there are only a select few (behind the curtains) who understand the secrets of how to make it all work compared to the billions of people who just consume YouTube videos (the outsiders). I hope my book will help level the playing field for those of you who are wondering how it all works.

I want to give you the power, the knowledge and the cold truth of how the game really works. How you can truly add value to the world, build a raving audience and make a fortune in the process.

I plan to reveal everything that I'm doing right now. This way, you can copy your way to success. Have you ever heard that quote "Success leaves trails?" I already did a lot of the failing, the hard work, all of the testing. In this book, I'm giving you what works. Are you ready? Ok great. Let's get cranking! And again, I want to thank you for joining me on this wonderful journey called life. Let's make your wildest dreams come true. You know that you can do it. I know that you can. I believe in you! Let's do it!

Table of Contents

Tube Cash

Introduction

"The journey of a thousand miles starts with one step at a time"
~ Lao Tzu ~

Listen, you've made a wise decision by joining me and reading this book today. I mean it.

In the first part of this book, I will introduce myself and tell my true story of how I started with a little bit of specialized knowledge in my head and turned it into a seven-figure online business.

By the time I was 16, I was a certified high school dropout. Then, long story short, I was forced to move to New York to live with my half-brother. My father convinced my mother that it was a good idea and that my older brother, who was 32 at the time, would straighten my ass out.

My brother John sat me down one night and gave me two options: (1) Work with him during the day while getting paid, and attend night school, get my GED and live rent free or (2) Work with him and not go to school and have to pay my own way with rent and other expenses. I proceeded with option 1, to work, get paid, and get my GED, what I call a "good enough diploma." I did that by the age of 17. I Moved back to Hawaii a year later to enroll myself in a local community college at 18, only to drop out twenty months later because I didn't want to take the recommended typing and public speaking classes. Crap! This sucks. Fast forward 10 years plus...

Now I run a completely mobile lifestyle business that I can run from anywhere in the world. Who would have known. Not me.

As I write this, I invite you to think differently. Look at this as your first step toward creating a new and fulfilled future where you can contribute value to the world and reap major benefits by doing so.

How does doing what you love, and having extra time, money and freedom sound to you?

Imagine running your own business while having more than enough cash-flow to support your family and lifestyle, plus having the ability to do this from anywhere in the world, 100% mobily.

When you create a low overhead cashflow business like the way I will be talking about, you'll be able to stash away thousands of dollars a month for other smart investments that will help you grow your wealth... sound amazing?

I thought so.

I also want to tell you what this book is and what it's not. Let's just make sure that you're in the right place with me here.

First, let me tell you what this book is *not*. This is not a get rich quick scheme. It's not a collection of made up stories, strategies and tactics that I've never personally used or experienced. This is not one of those push a button and get hordes of visitors to your website and make a ton of sales book.

Because frankly, you and I know that it's all BS. You're smarter than that. True success and true financial freedom takes work. It's not hard, it's simple. Yet, it's not easy, either.

I think the hardest part of it all is discipline and learning how to control yourself and your mind. That's why in this book you will see me get into the 'mind stuff' every once in a while.

I think there is a lack of this in most "how to make money online" courses out there today. Most of it is tech talk, how to create products, how to get traffic, etc....

But most people fail before they even get started. They fail because of not being clear on what they really want, by not being focused, not having a vision, having lack of confidence, having the fear of failure, having the fear of being judged by others, or because of low self-esteem and self-worth.

In this book, I will try to keep you pumped up, motivated and strong during the hard times, because I think we all could use some of that when times get tough. Especially when first starting out, or just lost in the abyss and paralyzed because of information overload.

It's Really Simple

Your #1 goal in ANY business is to create a win-win situation. Your customer gets what they want and are left extremely happy, and you being the fulfiller, get what you want by fulfilling, whether it be fulfilling digital products, access to your online courses, or delivering physical products or services.

The goal is the satisfaction of providing and delivering great products and turning a profit, which in turn, makes you and your company very happy. And it doesn't matter how big or small you are at this stage. I started as a one-man gang. Now I have a small team.

Note: I said the customer is extremely happy and you are happy. I think it's important to have repeat business. Then, you'll be extremely happy when your customers keep coming back for more. I think if you can accomplish that, then you've got something really good going for you.

Here's something else that you should take to heart and remember before I get into the meat of the matter. It'll be good food for thought for you to ponder on while you're on your journey to becoming a successful entrepreneur, and a self-made man or woman who's financially independent and prosperous.

Here it is...

Your ability to earn has nothing to do with your self-worth, your unique skills or your specialized knowledge.

And this is important to understand once you start making money with this. You will have your up's and down's. It's important that you learn to detach yourself emotionally from the attachment of thinking that your self-worth depends on your ability to earn. I think that your ability to earn is a skill-set of its own.

It doesn't matter if you physically work-out or not. It doesn't matter if you're a bad person or a good person. Your ability to earn is your most valuable asset no doubt, but it has no connection to your self-worth. You could have high self-worth and earn millions, or you could have low self-worth and still earn millions of dollars.

Here's the definition of self-worth by dictionary.com: "The sense of one's own value or worth as a person; self-esteem; self-respect."

You are unique. There is only one of you on earth. So, don't think you are worth less right now because you earn an average man's salary.

Example: Think of a college professor. Yes, he might be very intelligent, he has high self-worth, he is respected, and yes, he may be a good teacher, he may be likable, but... think about his *ability* to earn.

What is his personal *ability* to earn? He earns what the school pays him. The school and the system decides what he gets paid. He has no direct control over his income, therefore in my eyes, he has no personal *ability* to directly control what he earns in that position. There is a cap.

There is no unlimited earning potential for him unless he understands this and starts to position himself differently. He may be tenured and have the freedom of time for himself for study and to creating curriculums for his students. However, he does not have direct control of his *ability* to earn.

That's the amazing thing about the Tube-Cash business model that I'm about to share with you. You can grow this thing as big as you want, and the only thing that is stopping you is yourself and your limited beliefs. And I hope, with the help of this book, you can break out of the mould and truly be limitless. That is my goal for you!

Now let's talk about the same college professor. He has the same knowledge and the same self-worth, but rather than teaching at a college, he packages his teachings and put's it out to the mass market and he partners with the new online education services. He learns about marketing, networks with key companies and players and goes on to make millions of dollars. Ok, you may say, what if the professor is happy making his salary and working with students. What if he doesn't care about making more money? Well, I can assure you, maybe that guy is happy at where he is, but many other people would love to earn more money.

Same self-worth, but he now has the *ability* to earn more. Did you hear what I just said? He has the ABILITY TO EARN MORE. Now he makes ten times more. He learned and gained the ability to earn more. I hope this example drives it home for you.

And this is what you need to learn and improve on for yourself. You need to learn the ability to earn more. And you're just a few key skills away from doing so.

I highly encourage you to always be working on strengthening your self-worth as well as your *ability* to earn more. Once you are at the point where you feel comfortable at both, the world will truly be your oyster. And your ability to earn more just comes from learning, studying and applying marketing to your business, and that's what this book is all about!

Because whether you realize it or not, you've been marketing your entire life. The day you were born, you were actually selling. Think about it. You cried for milk. You sold yourself to your girlfriend/boyfriend or your spouse. Everyday you are buying and selling. Sell or be sold. If you want to make money, you need to sell. Period.

You need to make a promise to me right now. Promise to FOCUS and take ACTION. Take notes, reread chapters and learn. If you do that, you will start moving in the right direction, toward living the life of your dreams. If I, a high school drop-out with hardly any formal education can do it, so can you.

Just focus, learn and take action. That's the real secret. And I think you did just that by investing in this book.

Tony Richie

Chapter 1

How It All Started…

When I was in my early twenties, a girlfriend once told me that I needed a real job. I was always buying and selling cars and working with my dad at his automotive shop just doing my own thing to make money. She was like, "You're not even paying taxes. Get a real job!" Back then, I will admit, I was mostly in the cash business and wasn't up to date with the tax law. But since I liked her, I decided to get a job at a local Japanese Yakiniku restaurant. Yakiniku in Japanese is the style of food where they, the cooks, cook meats in front of you. You can also do it yourself if you go to that type of restaurant. Long story short, the job lasted 5 months, and so did the rest of our relationship.

So, I can truthfully say that I tried working for someone once, it wasn't for me, and I never tried it again.

I guess I come by my entrepreneurial tendencies honestly. My father comes from a construction and automotive background. He moved to Hawaii in 1975 from Long Island New York, where he decided to open his own automotive shop.

I grew up hanging around the shop part-time, only because my parents got divorced when I was seven. But over the years, almost everything I learned about cars, I learned from my dad.

I learned how to fix them mechanically. I learned how to do body work and paint. I also even went to technical college to learn about the automotive industry. I was just shy of getting my degree because I didn't want to finish typing class and the required speech class, so I dropped out of college. And now I've already spoken at the Harvard Business Faculty Club about marketing and YouTube and also appeared in a handful of local news channels. Go figure.

When I was in my early twenties, I made most of my money buying and selling cars. I would go to auctions and re-do the cars that I bought. I would paint them, fix up the engines, and then sell them for a profit. I was a total car nut. I still am, but right now, I don't need to work on them to make money anymore. Now I teach people how to repair and fix cars. That's how I make my money. I also sell a lot physical items like tools and materials in the automotive space. This is why I am so excited to share all of this with you. Because once you understand how it all works, you can sell anything online.

The Beginning

When I was twenty-five I got married and then I experienced my first true defining moment. I had a baby girl on the way and when she was born, I knew that I had to really rethink my future. Some nights my wife and I would have long conversations and one night we were talking about online marketing. I knew nothing about it, neither did she, but I was starting to get an idea of how it all worked by browsing the net, reading and watching videos... Weeks later my wife said, "Hey Tony, why don't you start uploading videos and showing people what you know?"

I said what? .... She said "Why don't you take what you know, and just start putting it online?" I was a little reluctant at first because I was such a computer dunce... but after a week or so of just thinking about it, I just started doing. I didn't know what I was doing, I was just doing! And that should be a big takeaway for you. It's better to do something and do it wrong, then do nothing at all. At least you'll learn something by taking that action.

So, I started to put up little YouTube videos, helping people and giving tips about cars and how to get the best deal when buying a car. Easy little tips that were only three to five minute videos.

I was sharing tips and tricks from my own experience, from my dad, and also from other information that I found online. I also learned a lot from courses and some paid seminars that I attended through my years about cars.

I started to put what I knew on the internet. I first organized what specialized knowledge I had inside of my head (formal and non-formal) and I started to put this content out into the web through articles, blogs, posting on forums and some video posting on sites like Vimeo, DailyMotion and of course, YouTube.

I was putting everything that I was learning about online marketing into action and eventually, 6 months or so later, all these articles and videos that I was putting up started to get a lot of views, which is called 'traffic' in online marketing terms. Not a ton, but enough to create a dialog with my viewers and email subscribers.

I was only uploading about 1-2 videos a week. Not much at all because I had no Idea how I would benefit or how it would evolve. I had no idea of the impact and leverage these videos would later provide me.

While I was doing all of this, we were renting the bottom part of my mother's house in Hawaii. I was twenty-six years old, freshly married, with a newborn baby. This was literally the fire under my butt saying, "Hey, Tony. You have to do something different if you want different results."

Either you're going to have your own physical car repair shop and work on cars for the rest of your life as a J.O.B. or, you're going to take a leap of faith, believe in yourself and attack something new and expect different results.

Tube Cash

I've seen how much work my father put in with the car business and I've seen the conditions. Dealing with customers just wasn't something I wanted to do as a day to day job. I had already been dealing with customers and I knew the game. I was doing it since I was seventeen.

So, with my wife's help and learning through online courses and investing in programs about marketing and selling online, I was putting all of these articles and videos up and I started to get massive results. It just started growing and growing, and I literally started all of this out of my mother's two car garage.

While all this was taking off for me, my father sat me down one day and said, "Listen, I'm going to close up the shop." He was sixty-eight at that time and he said, "Do you want to take over the business? If you want, I'll hand it over to you and you can run it." We had a lot of clientele and it was a money-making business. But I told him, "I don't want to do it." He said, "Fine, no problem son." He then sold the shop and his entire business.

Like I said, my vision wasn't running a repair shop. I just had a new baby and I focused on putting everything online. I wanted to be mobile and have a business that was going with the trend. I wanted to create an online course that taught people how to learn about cars and restore them because that's what I grew up with. That's what I knew.

So, that's what I did. And it became the world's most popular online DIY course with high schools in Austin, TX and in Canada using my curriculum in their classes. I even had a New Mexico State penitentiary use the courses to teach their inmates a new vocational skill set. Pretty amazing if you ask me!

And when I said I literally started filming out of my mother's two-car garage, that's what I did! I went to Home Depot and spent a little over eighty dollars. I bought four gallons of paint and painted inside of the garage white so it looked nice and clean. I painted the floor, so when I did my filming it didn't look bad. I worked with what I had. I didn't worry saying, "My garage is too small, or I don't have the proper camera equipment, and yada yada yada…"

I also started with a ninety-nine dollar Kodak Zi8 video camera, which didn't even have an automatic zoom, so when I had to zoom up on something I had to manually flip a switch to get the zoom working. It was crazy.

Within my first twelve months of setting everything up, I did over a hundred and fifty thousand dollars in sales online and most of it was profit because as you know it's very inexpensive to run an online business, especially if your main products are digitally fulfilled. I did this completely on my own, all automated through my websites and it was amazing. A year after that, it blew up even bigger. Within the first two years, I did well over four hundred thousand dollars in sales online. It was an amazing ride. We surpassed the one million dollars in sales mark within the next twelve months after that.

And it all started with simple home-made videos, out of my mother's garage, just by sharing what I knew. I see no reason why you can't do the same. I'm about to lay it all out for you in plain English. I want to show you exactly how you can do this because really, it isn't complicated. I think the hardest part of it is convincing yourself that you can do it, and believing in yourself that you can do it and of course, just taking action and doing it.

Remember, I didn't graduate college. I don't have any formal degrees. However, I did attend a special trade class to get a mini certificate if I thought it would benefit me and add to my credentials. I started using these little credentials that I earned, plus all the experience, and I backpacked off my father who was in the business for thirty years.

I have been working on cars since I was fourteen. I was working on cars and basically used all of that to my advantage, to start promoting what I knew best.

You can do the same thing. It doesn't matter where you're starting out or how much experience you have right now. You can always go out and learn more. Positioning yourself and your product is something that you create for yourself.

You create the vision that you want people to see. It's a powerful thing and I want to show you exactly how to do all of this. Now you may feel like… "well Tony, I don't have any special skill or I'm not good at anything. How can I start an online business like you?"

Well, the answer is simple, and it may be a little too simple. So simple that you may just push me off and take what I say for granted. But don't. Really think about what I'm about to write down on this page.

Your new job is to solve problems. If you don't know where to start, start with yourself. Take inventory of yourself. What kind of problem are you experiencing right now? Are you looking to get into better shape? Are you struggling with procrastination? Heck …that sounds like a product to me! "ProcrastinationCures.com." The next step is to learn all you can about the topic, not too hard because it only takes a few weeks of research, some books and understanding to become pretty knowledgeable in something. And it helps if you're like me and already have something that you can use and provide value to others with. Of course, when you practice what you preach and start to get results for yourself, then you're on to the holy grail. For example, when you see these guys who lose all of this weight and come out with a rock-solid body, if they did it right and documented the process and wrote down what he ate, how he worked out, discussed his daily routine... do you see how this could be put into a book/video course and sold as a weight loss product online? People are doing this daily and you don't even need to create and sell your own products, if you get up and going, you can start promoting other people's products and making a commission on products sold.

Next, after you decide the topic that you will be sharing your experiences and value with the market, start talking about your experience on social networks and open a YouTube account. Because there is a right way and a wrong way of getting setup on YouTube, I will show you the right way of getting setup on YouTube at www.tonyrichie.com/bookbonus. You definitely don't want to start off on the wrong foot.

Talk about your struggle, your successes and everything in between. Once you start doing that you'll automatically start attracting a crowd, your own audience. Once you do this, all you need to do is grow it. Keep pushing out content. And remember that content is not king. Distribution is king! You need to get your message out and heard to make any difference in the lives of others and in yours. From there, I'll show you how to package and sell your own simple products 100% online! That's it! And you can do this in virtually any niche market! isn't this exciting?!? Moving on...

So, this was a quick story of how I started and what I do to make an unbelievable income online. Now it's your turn. Follow me on to chapter two and let's get clear on what you want out of life and why you want it. It's important.

Tube Cash

Chapter 2

Creating Your Dream Day
and Living Life on Your Own Terms...

Imagine waking up... and it's your ideal day. You don't have to worry about money because you know you have an online business that's open and working for you 24/7, 365 days a year.

You have customers that are available all around the world. Geographical locations don't matter and you can run this business from anywhere around the world. You could be in Mexico on the beach, or in Japan, like I am right now...

Your websites are accepting payments and you're making sales effortlessly, even while you sleep.

Just imagine being able to travel around the world and taking your family with you, experiencing different cultures, places and languages.

Imagine not being tied down to a regular nine to five job or answering to a boss who doesn't respect you and your family.

How different would your life be if you had no ties to a regular nine to five job? How would it feel? What would you do differently?

I never knew there was a world like this before I started online marketing. I was probably in a position like you where I was working for money, and trading time for money. Like I say, most people are too busy earning a living to actually live and enjoy life. So let's solve this issue now!

I never knew there was a world out there where I could have automation and systems working for me 24/7 taking orders and making me money while I sleep.

This is the reality that I live in right now and I want you to experience the same, if you would like that, and honestly, who wouldn't?

It's a truly fulfilling when you start to experience a life like this. Many times, when I'm on a flight I have to turn my cellphone to airplane mode, I'm always excited to see how much money I made when I turn my phone back on.

It's an amazing and addicting feeling once you have these systems up and working for you. I never thought this was all possible until I learned about the internet and how to provide value in exchange for money.

I want you to be able to do the same exact thing.

What This Can Do For You?

This can give you freedom like no other. Imagine being able to take off from work for a week or two, without asking for permission? The income still comes in.

The harder you work, the more you will be rewarded, but if something happens unexpectedly and you have to take a week off, or if you have to travel, the money will still come in.

There are months at a time where I just couldn't be physically managing my business, but the business still runs on its own.

You could have a support agent helping you out and you could be totally absent from it, but the business still runs. You still bring in income, which is a fabulous way of living. It can free up time for you, for your family, and allow you to live mobile from anywhere in the world.

One thing that you will gain, that I think even money can't buy, is the true peacefulness and freedom of being self-sufficient, self-made and knowing that you are going to be okay. Waking up in the morning, seeing a thousand or two thousand dollars in sales overnight you know that it's going to be okay.

As long as you keep following the proven system and growing your business, things are going to be okay, because you are on a trend that is only getting bigger and bigger. But you need to remember that you must work *on* your business, and not *in* your business. You need to set up automation and hire help when the time is right. I'll share with you how I did that in the beginning.

What Will Happen If You Don't Take Action?

If you don't take action, a year or two from now, you're going to be in the same position you're in right now. You're not going to have an online business. You're won't have the opportunity to gain freedom. You're not going to have the lifestyle and do whatever the heck you want.

You'll be stuck in the same cycle, the circle of the rat race, wishing that you'd started a few years before. You'll probably be sitting right there thinking to yourself, "Man, I should have gotten started when I read Tony's book." You'll be regretting that you should have started sooner. You're still going to be locked in to the nine-to five job. Nothing's going to change.

Your family will be older, you'll be older. In fact, it could even be a little worse, and I don't want you to feel that way or get into that sort of situation.

But what if things could be worlds better?

If you don't take action, the only person to blame is yourself because you are responsible for the current situation and outcome in your life.

You are responsible for the way you're living your life right now. Sit down and look all around you right now … Your cars, your house, your family life, your social life with your family and with people you associate with – friends or business partners. You are responsible for all of that. For things to change, you need to change.

You need to change the way you think, you need to change the way you eat, you need to change the way you treat each other, you need to change the way you feed your brain and how you look at opportunities.

If something bad happens in life, try not to look at the negative. Look for the solution. A lot of people tend to focus on the negative immediately, and yes, I get it, I am guilty at that too, but I remind myself and correct myself as soon as I catch myself going negative. I would say that 99% of the people focus on the negative as soon as something happens instead of thinking of a solution to the problem. Start thinking solutions and positive things that you can do to overcome those situations.

Think how can I get around it? How can I overcome it? How can I beat it? What is the good out of this situation?

Sometimes, the good doesn't show up immediately, but if you keep thinking about the good and how you can overcome and make things better, that's the way to go because your mind is forced to open and to think.

Believe it or not, our minds and our brains are the middle man to the universe of infinite intelligence. It's very, very important to think positive, rather than negative.

What will happen if you don't take action? The simple answer is *nothing*. You need to change in order to expect different results, so let's step out of your comfort zone and let's get started.

By stepping out of your comfort zone you, too, can have your ideal dream day and I don't even want to call it a job, because it really isn't. Wouldn't you like to make hundreds, or even thousands of dollars just by sitting on an airplane, or walking around Disney World with your kids, or visiting the Imperial Palace in Tokyo?

I've been fortunate (because of taking action) to be able to live my dream day every day, and I am here to help you live yours, too.

I want to share with you something very special in this chapter and you will need to go to my site to get it. This one thing changed my life when I learned as I was getting started online and I think it was one of the biggest factors of my success.

This is not my formula so I can't take 100% credit for it, but I did change it up a little and made my own version so to say. I call it the M.F.N. What is the MFN?

Well, once you complete the first part of this exercise, you'll have a clear vision on how much money you need to start earning right now to set yourself free from your current work/job. This way you'll have complete control and freedom to go all in on your new venture once you're able to do that.

Part two is having a clear goal and vision on what you need financially to live your dream lifestyle. And this is what made me stay up late at nights to continue to work on my project and deadlines. Even when the times got tough, I kept my mind on what I wanted and eventually I got it.

I want to share this MFN exercise with you right now so please go to: **www.TonyRichie.com/bookbonus** and enter your full name and email to get access to this special gift. Put in 20-30 minutes right now and complete the exercise. You'll be glad that you did. I am telling you, this one thing changed my life forever. Do it now and come back to this book.

Chapter 3

YouTube:
Your Very Own Billion Dollar Distribution Channel!

It was late 2009, and I was getting into internet marketing and learning how to create and sell digital/physical products online. I was like, wow this is amazing! That's when I discovered Mike Filsaime, Jim Edwards and all these other gurus and known copywriters like Gary Halbert and Joe Sugarman. At first I just wanted to make money online. I just wanted to sell "how to make money online," It was obvious that the guys who knew what they were doing were making a lot of money, but the issue was, I didn't know how to make money online!

My wife later said, "Why don't you just start with what you know?" I'm like, "What do you mean? What do I do?" She said, "You're into cars! You love cars, you know a lot about cars. Why don't you just start doing stuff online about cars?" I thought it made perfect sense so that's exactly what I did, and I started making homemade videos and then uploading them to YouTube. I knew that video was a growing trend, and was bound to only get bigger. Today, it's a powerhouse that you simply can't ignore. Today if you plan to build an online business, you need to be using some kind of video in your marketing.

So, back to the story... At that time, I was working with my mom and step-father, seven days a week for the first year, helping her open her new food shop. I was up at 4:00 in the morning, and by noon I was done. The rest of the day was for me. I was basically my mother's delivery guy, delivering food to all these different stores during the day. In between, while I was driving, I'd make videos talking about cars. Initially, how to find cars and how to buy and sell cars, inspection tips for buying cars for profit, just everything about cars. I started uploading videos to YouTube without thinking much of it. I wasn't expecting much in return. I was just thinking to myself, let me just get stuff out there, get content out there. I knew that content was king. But later I discovered that the combination of good content and a solid distribution medium was king. If you put out good content, then people were going to watch it, like it, share it, and subscribe, etc.

Six to eight months later I started getting a ton of comments and people were subscribing and asking for more videos. That's when I decided to create my first product which taught people how to find good car deals. I followed the marketing advice of what was working at that time and created a little sales funnel. With my first product launch online, I did $4,500 out of the gate within my first 2 weeks! Pretty good considering that I was only getting paid $1,500 a month helping my mom at the restaurant working 7 days a week. So in essence, in one day I tripled my income. And I did it with a small email subscriber list from YouTube. By the way, it was a life changing day for me! I then celebrated with my whole family. Champagne was on me! I knew that life was never to be the same.

Becoming a Self-Made YouTube Star (in a small little niche) - And The Power of Habits...

I got started with YouTube by sharing my homemade videos. They were bad. I was stuttering in a lot of the videos, saying the word "okay" too much. My videos were so bad in the beginning that people were teasing me on YouTube, like putting "okay, okay, okay..." in the comments section because I said "okay" too much in my video. Obviously, I wasn't emulating anyone in my videos. I was just being myself. And I think that's what really worked. I realized that in order to really build a tribe you had to be real.

It had to be Tony on those videos, including all the stuttering and "okays," not some made-up character. You just have to be yourself. That was who I was, and the somewhat polished person that you see in my videos today is what I matured into, and it's still me. In the eyes of others, I probably still have many flaws… but who's perfect anyway? Just be YOU.

It didn't matter that I stuttered or made mistakes or had people poke fun at me, because people still subscribed and they will do the same to you, too. Obviously, people liked my videos because they were becoming fans and buying my products.

Once I saw what was working, I just did more of it. I just started uploading videos every week.

All of this was happening when my father decided to sell his business. After he did that, I didn't have an automotive shop anymore to actually start making my content videos. Before that, I never made videos because I never knew this world of online marketing even existed. Plus, YouTube wasn't even around when I was a hard-core car repair guy.

Prior to discovering all of this, I never recorded any of the jobs that I did on automotive work, like a step by step video or any kind of series. I should have, but at that time I didn't do it. I only took some pictures and that's what I started to share on YouTube, a series of before and after photos of my work in the shop.

As I was getting into this, I had no shop, and no real location. I could have rented a place, but I was cash strapped at that point and it didn't make sense for me to do so. I had a new baby on the way, and I didn't want to rent a shop for $2,500 a month. I thought that if I did that I'd be trapped in the rat race, worrying about doing customer jobs just to pay the rent and I was not going to do that.

So, I recorded my first instructional video series working on a car in my mother's garage at home, with my ninety-nine dollar video camera. I recorded videos and uploaded them to YouTube as well as the more in-depth videos for my online membership site (where I planned to make the real money) and sell my product.

I put the members course together within twelve weeks and launched it late one night as I was working with my overseas Pakistani developers. It was literally 2 AM on a Friday night and I was so tired, I just called it a night. When I woke up the next morning, I was so excited to check my stats. I had only slept about 4 hours because I was so excited to see if I made any sales. And lo and behold... there was $1,476 and change sitting in my shopping cart account. And this was just overnight, a few hours after I sent out my first email!

I couldn't believe it. It was the best day of my life. I did it! I made money online! I sold my own products through an email list I built and built a relationship with through YouTube. I sold my products. It worked!

I wanted to celebrate! I decided to take my wife and new baby girl M, who was about 15 months old at the time, and my dad out for breakfast that morning. We had pancakes and eggs over at an old-time pancake house called "The Original Pancake House" off Dillingham Blvd in Honolulu. It's still there today. You should go one day!

By the end of the month I did $4,500 in sales, selling a $147.00 lifetime membership course on how to repair cars. Not too bad considering that we were already half way through the month.

After that initial success, I was addicted. There was no looking back. I knew that this was how I wanted to make a living from now on. I had two of my own automotive products out now and two YouTube channels getting views and sending my website targeted visitors. All I had to do was to keep making more videos so people could discover what I was putting out. My videos would show them how they could modify or fix their cars. My videos would inspire and motivate people to realize that they could do it and get awesome results like I did.

History was made. I kept learning everything I could about YouTube, sales funnels, and marketing. The most important part was that I consistently put to action what I learned. Not only did I continuously study marketing, but I also kept personal development close to my soul as I believe nothing is harder to master than yourself. It's a constant challenge even for successful people to stay focused on what they are truly striving for. You need to have a vision, and you need to set goals and deadlines to hit them.

But I do think it gets easier when success literally becomes habit. If you focus enough and reward yourself when you get things done and accomplished (it's best to do this daily), over time your habits will change and you will become a permanent success. Until then, keep setting high goals 3-6 months out, and strive to reach them. Don't forget your daily and weekly goals as well. This will keep you on track to hit your 3-6 month targets. As you accomplish and bang out your daily and weekly targets, reward yourself - be it a cup of coffee, a great dinner out, a totally non-work and fun day with the family, etc.

Getting important things done and rewarding yourself afterward is the perfect "cue and reward" factor that will help your brain create a habit. Once you create these success habits, nothing will stop you. For more information about habits and how powerful habits are, check out this book that I recommend on my book bonus page at: **www.TonyRichie.com/bookbonus.**

The 2 Ways You Can Make Money With YouTube

I read an article that said, "YouTube is the new TV network."

It's literally taking over. YouTube reaches more of the millennial generation than TV right now. You should also know that the millennials, are the largest US generation in history, larger than the Baby Boomer generation. They are the next big spenders.

I remember when as a kid the TV set had a dial with 13 channels in UHF on it. Networks held all of the power to get into people's homes and you didn't have much choice when it came to what you wanted to watch.

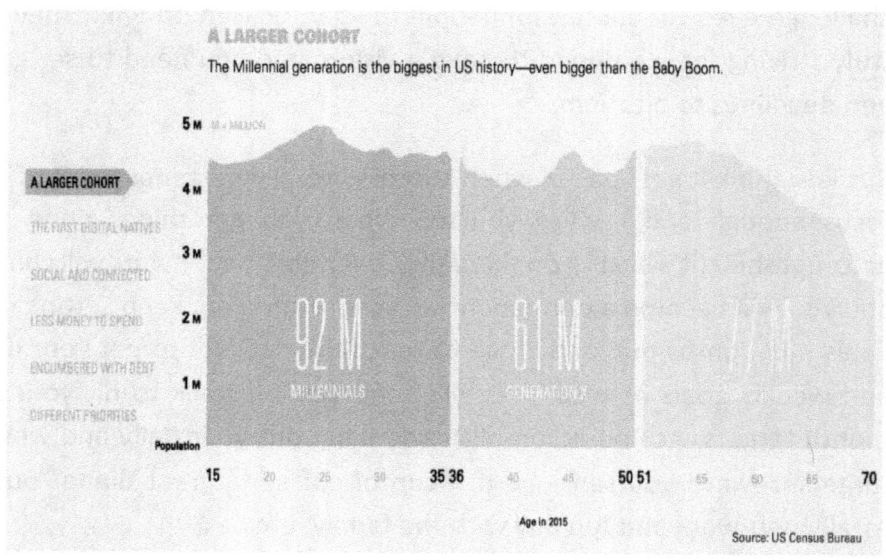

Now YouTube has shared that power with everybody, and YouTube's not even a network. However, my channel on YouTube is a network, and yours can be, too! I control most of the programming and commercials. If I want to make money off videos, I just enable monetization in the backend of my YouTube account and viola! I now make money when people watch my videos.

Many people don't know how people make money with YouTube and I'm about to reveal to you the two main ways people can make money with YouTube below. If you want to learn this in a more detailed fashion over some personal training videos that I created, please don't forget to check out my book bonus page at **www.TonyRichie.com/bookbonus.**

With that said, here are the two ways you can make money with YouTube:

1: **Become a YouTube partner**. Say what? "You become a YouTube partner." So what is a YouTube partner and how does it work? How do you make money that way?

Here it is. When you're on YouTube watching a video, have you ever seen those ads on the top right next to the video? Those banners? Have you ever seen those small google banner ads within the video toward the bottom? Have you ever seen the in-stream video ad commercial being played (that you have to click to skip) in order to watch the video that you intended to watch?

As you know, those are ads, and if you click on them or not, the video creator (the person who made the video that you're planning to watch) gets paid a small percentage because those ads were served by or within their video. As a YouTube partner, you can enable monetization after you verify your new YouTube channel and or website with Google. When that feature is enabled, you can allow your video to be monetized and (you can make money from ad revenue) by your videos being played and watched.

Cool! So how does this work? The advertiser, the company that is paying for the ad to be there (in the form of a banner or an in-stream video) is paying YouTube to show and serve those ads. Because they are serving ads over your content (your video) YouTube splits the ad revenue with you. As of now it's a 55/45 split and you get paid on a CPM basis. CPM = Cost per 1,000 impressions. An impression is each time an ad is loaded and displayed on a page, whether a person sees it or not. The reason why a person may not see it is because it loads below the fold of the page.

What does "Above the fold, and Below the fold" mean? if you're on a website that just loaded, whatever you see without scrolling down is called above the fold. If you need to scroll down to see the rest of the page, that's called below the fold.

There are YouTube partners out there making five figures to as much as seven figures a month through this method of monetizing their videos and being a YouTube partner. In order to be successful with this method on YouTube, you need a lot of views, and I mean a lot. One of my smaller channels on YouTube currently only gets about 50,000 video views a month across all of my videos combined which results in about $200.00 - $300.00 per month in my share of ad money. Not too shabby for some side money, but nothing that you can totally live off. Some of my other larger channels on YouTube earn in excess of a few thousand dollars per month. Yes, it can be enough to live off, but it's nothing substantial to where you could live your dream life and travel the world. I see this money as extra free money. that I can use to invest in my business to grow it bigger. The guys on YouTube who are getting millions of views a month are the ones making more or better money through the YouTube partner program.

In order to be really successful in that style of monetization, you need a very large viewership/audience, hundreds of thousands of subscribers, and basically you need to be uploading a video to YouTube at least 5 times per week, if not daily. Just look at the most successful YouTubers - they're doing a video a day and have been doing so for quite some time.

Later in the book I will give you the #1 trick to really making it on YouTube and a few other golden rules that you can use with whatever method you decide to use to make money.

I will now cover the second way you can make money with YouTube and it's the way I use YouTube to make millions of dollars in my businesses. The crazy thing is that you can't tell from the outside because you don't need a lot of views to make a lot of money this way.

2. Niche down and create niche audiences. Specialize on a certain topic, deliver value, create a tribe and you can sell your own products and services, or sell affiliate products if you don't have any product to sell in the beginning.

YouTube is a goldmine for doing this and not many people are successfully doing it (mostly because they have no idea of how to). Honestly, I only know of a handful of people, including myself, who are absolutely crushing it by applying this method.

This will work for you if you have specialized knowledge that people are seeking for, whether it be legal advice, real estate tips, pet care, home repair, travel blogging, dentistry, personal development, or virtually anything else. You can do this in thousands of niches and topics. Were you a professional at your job for something? Have you mastered small business management? Do you know all there is to know about sailboats and sailing? Are you an expert on a certain hobby? Sports? Collectables? Know how to rebuild engines? Are you a lawn expert? Are you a great speaker and would like to start your own business teaching others how to effectively speak? I can go on and on... and I'm sure you can too.

You're probably thinking, "Well, Tony, I'm really not an expert in anything. So, what do I do?" This, I believe is just a case of limited thinking. So many people give up before they even get started... don't let that be you. You need to think, "Well, how could I become better at what I do, what can help me be viewed as an expert?"

I heard a marketer say this once and it stuck to me. You only need to know a little more than the person who is buying your product. If you're selling something that's helping somebody accomplished their mission, or solve their problem, then you've rendered a service. And it only helps that once you decide on a topic to create a business around, to continue to learn more about it as you go on. You know, they say the best way to learn something new is to learn it for yourself, and teach at the same time. it's simple. Further down in the book I will dive deeper on this subject but let's get back on track of how this business model works.

With the second method of making money off YouTube, all you do is put out great free information about the topic that you decided on and love to talk about, create and upload a video at least once a week. 2-3 videos a week would be better, but the main point is to just get started on the idea. Don't worry if you think you're not good enough, or not good on camera… your mind will automatically play tricks on you when you're getting out of your comfort zone and trying get something new going. You'll start to gain more confidence as you keep moving forward. Just do it.

Once you start putting out great information on your chosen topic the way I show you, you'll start to position yourself as an expert in your marketplace. As you do that, get a simple website built (like I show you how to easily setup inside of my advanced trainings) then people will be giving you their email for more information to learn more about you and your products. Just like I am doing here. Awesome, isn't it?

As you do this you'll start to build a list of people who are interested on the topic that you're talking about. Next, your simple selling system will do all of the hard work for you. To do this you'll get setup with your very own email marketing software that will help you automate most of your emails and product delivery. This may seem complicated if you're new to this idea. But, it's a proven model that has generated billions of dollars online and off. It's called direct response marketing, but we're doing it online instead of offline. Please remember that if I can do it, a technical dunce with no formal education, you can.

By far I think this is the best way to make money online, especially when you harness the power of video and YouTube. Not many people are doing it successfully. And the best part is, you don't need a lot of views to make a large income because your views are so targeted to people who are only interested in that subject and I will show you how to hook them in and turn them into a loyal subscriber and customer of yours.

As you do this and put into action what I'm teaching you, through your message and how you structure your videos, you will leave your viewers wanting more. They will then funnel over to your site to learn more about you and your products and some of them will eventually buy from you. This method is the second way to make money with YouTube and online period. You need to remember that YouTube is just a distribution channel for you to get out there and discovered online. You can do the same with basic article marketing, and using other channels such as Instagram, Twitter, niche topic forums, Facebook, Pinterest and others. But when getting started I suggest to start with two to three main platforms or else it will be too much to manage unless you have a helper/virtual assistant. Again, out of all of the platforms above, I know that YouTube is a must. Video content and distribution is king.

You can also use both methods to make money on YouTube like I do. I make money selling my own information products in a few different markets as well as from the YouTube ad revenue, from being a YouTube partner.

You hear that a zillion people every day watch YouTube. I don't really care how many people are on YouTube. I only care how many people are watching my videos, watching my channel and this is how you should be thinking as well. Let's get your channel up and running! Don't forget to get more in-depth training and bonuses from this book at my site: www.TonyRichie.com/bookbonus

Ready to rock and roll? Let's get deeper into building your micro niche tube cash machine in the next chapter.

Chapter 4

How-To Dominate Your Space,
Even If You Suck At It...

Micro niches are a great way to build a loyal tribe and a business. You can inject your real personality and dominate the market. Once you get a foothold it's easy to expand and widen your niche, introduce new products and even get into selling physical products. In my how-to videos on YouTube, I show how people to fix a dent, how to feather a panel, how to paint a panel. It would just be content, content, content. But what I've come to find that works even better is every fourth or fifth video, weave in your personal lifestyle. Show you kid, your pet, just talk about the topic and be you, show your life a little. People love that.

Weave in a talk about your family, what you did last weekend, your real life, what you're doing... we went on vacation, we did this and this. I even let my kids get in my video occasionally. They say hi, and people like that. They like to see that I'm a family man. "His daughter's cute," I get comments like that, just by putting my kids in my video. It's important to not just be exclusive to content because it can get boring. Weave in your real personality as well and try to make it fun and of course, it's supposed to be fun!

With social media, it's all about connecting. It's not some paid actor standing up there in a polished studio with professional lighting and the whole works. That's not what people want. They want the real deal.

As an example, when people are getting into their passion, or they're learning about something, they're micro niching down. They've found something they want to share, and once you start sharing those things it's easy to learn more and share, putting your own twist on it also makes it cooler. It's continuously learning. If you want to expand, expand however deep and wide you want to go. Remember I said, the best way to learn is to learn and teach it right after you learn it. So if you feel that you're pretty knowledgeable in a niche market, share it, but it doesn't mean that you're done. Learn more about your own topic as you go, create new videos and share and sooner than later, you'll really start to look like the expert.

For those of you reading this book who don't know anything about micro niches, information marketing, selling information online or offline, it's all basically the same thing. It's just the means of advertising a product or service and delivering. It's never been easier to start a business like this. And it is a true lifestyle business that you can run from the comfort of your own home. You'll get to live anywhere and earn everywhere.

Information marketing has been around for hundreds of years. People who always sell information, especially accurate and helpful information to the public, are invaluable.

Basically, all you're doing is packaging what you know and selling it to the world. I know that this is a broad overview, but it's really simple, especially with the access to so many online tools, technology and software that we have at our fingertips nowadays.

It's very easy to find and serve a hungry market. With the online tools that we use, we can see what people are searching for and what they need. We can even start a dialogue with them - this way we can create and sell them exactly what they want. This insures us in advance that you have a market that's going to buy your product before you even create it.

I can virtually guarantee that there are people in hundreds of niches all around the world that are interested in weird things that you probably don't have any idea about. Now you may be thinking, "Well,

Tony, I'm not really an expert in anything. What do I sell" Before I answer that question, keep reading.

Let me give you a couple of examples. For me, I started in the automotive market, but health is another huge one. When you think of the health market, there are tons of different angles that you can come off from. You can go into weight loss, certain types of diets – the Paleo diet, low carb diet, low fat diet, the organic food diet, the greens only diet... there are just so many angles that you can take, It's really limitless, and that's not even talking about cross promoting different products to your audience.

Basically, what we do here is take what you know, do more extensive research, find out what the market wants. If you're in the animal market, you'll want to find out exactly what your audience wants by simply asking them.

Then we create your product, we create a little three to five-page website, put a BUY NOW button on it and send some targeted people over to it. Again, you're probably asking "Tony, how do I get interested people in that market over to my site to buy my products?" Great question, because that's where my *TubeCashSystem* comes in. It will be your goldmine for this. And I can show you how this is done over video. Just remember to go to **www.TonyRichie.com/bookbonus** to get that information.

For now, here's how it's done step-by-step in text format. You'll start off by putting out your video content out on YouTube in your desired market. As an example, you would create a little video that says, "Ten Tips To Potty Train Your Animal." Maybe you show them how to use special cookies and a special scent spray to make it all work. So in your video you show them the tips. You say something like "Hey, this is how you reward them with a cookie when they do it right and this is the spray that you want to use on their little pee pad." They go there, they smell it and they go to the bathroom. Boom, they are potty trained.

Now here's where you can buy the product. You show them a little three to five-minute tutorial on how it all works and then direct them to your site to buy the physical or digital products. Get the idea? Great!

Then you would expand on your keywords over multiple targeted videos. This is how you can target different dog breeds. You can say German Shepherd potty training, Doberman potty training... Of course, you would make the title a lot more appealing so people gain curiosity, click on it and watch the video.

This is how you drive targeted people who are on the internet searching for, "How do I train my German Shepherd?" Like, "How do I potty train my German Shepherd?"

They're searching online through Google or YouTube or wherever they are and they end up on your video. Your video teaches them, "Hey, this is how you do it and these are the special cookies we sell." Or this is the dog training program that we offer. But there is a small step before directly selling them a product, it's called a lead magnet. And I will cover this more in-depth for you further in the book. I am just getting you primed up right now.

That's how you get targeted people to see your stuff. It's as simple as that. The way to get a lot of traffic online is to have free content videos out there doing all of the work for you that help people with their problems by offering them solutions.

For example, on one of my YouTube channels, I have close to five hundred videos in the car industry. I know it seems like a lot, but this is after years of adding videos. Again, I started with one video a week and eventually started to do more as my business grew. You can do the same.

The more you add, the bigger and bigger your audience will get. When I say audience, I mean the crowd, your subscribers that watch your videos, the people who follow you, the new people that will be constantly finding your content videos though online searches. And they will find you because you're smart and you're doing it the *"Tony Richie"* way. The proven way because you know that I do this to make a lot of money. I am not one of those guru guys who just makes money teaching this stuff. I do it every day.

You do this, and you'll get more and more traffic, and you'll get it organically. Organically means when you create good content videos, YouTube and Google will rank your content for free at the top of the search engines. If you search how to potty train a German Shepherd, your video will be at the very top. You're not paying to be there. The same thing in Google - you're at the very top without paying. That's organic traffic, organic rankings. Now remember, you don't need to be #1 to do well in this. My content and sites are all over YouTube and Google and I am not necessarily #1 for all of my main search terms and keywords. There will be some videos that will make it higher in the search, and some that don't. It all works out. The aim is to just get the content out. There are steps that you can take to increase your chances to rank higher which in return will get you more organic views and will lead to more visitors to your website. But because you're following my video ranking formula that I've tested and perfected over the years, you'll have a much better chance in dominating the keywords and niche markets that you decide to go after.

This is a very powerful way to get your free content out into the internet. The cool thing is that you can use more than one distribution method to do this. YouTube is a distribution channel along with Google, Facebook,

Twitter, and Instagram, which are all ways to get your information out to the world. They are all distribution channels that can work for you when building your business. There are so many, but when first starting out, I would highly recommend to start with two or three at the most. The worst thing to do when getting started is to thin your efforts out.

I really, strongly recommend using video as one way to get your content out, and you'll do this by using YouTube. The facts are there. Everything is video right now and it's going to continue to be video. Then I would add another channel to your mix. Maybe you already have a Facebook following, twitter or Instagram. If you do, I would use what you have right now. If you are doing something that's very image related, something that people need to see, I would suggest using Instagram or Pinterest.

If you want to get a lot of people to see your message and it's something the masses are interested about, and it has a possibility of going viral. Yes, Facebook has video, but it can't compete with what YouTube has going for it. YouTube is simply the gorilla online when it comes to people searching for content and how-to information to solve their problems and for basic entertainment of course.

To start off on the right foot, you want to make sure that you upload at the least, a video a week, or if you're ambitious like I was, then upload two to three videos a week.

Some guys out there are doing a video a day. How long does it take to create a video? You record a five-minute video, teaching a certain tip and you upload it and put it out there. It only takes a half hour to put something together and upload it. Not long at all. If you're serious about this and you want it bad, do it.

If you sit down a few nights a week, you can easily write out a marketing plan, a content strategy so you know what you need to do once a week or twice a week or more. You can prepare for it and get everything going.

Start off by marketing what you know by putting free content out on the internet to gain traffic. That's one of the main things. Just get started. This is what I did. This part is not rocket science. It's basically you doing something and getting started.

If you don't get eyeballs to your website, to your offers and products, nothing is going to happen. This is the main idea of an online business. You need to make sure that you can funnel targeted people over to your website so they can see what you have to offer in exchange for money.

The other way is to buy ads online which results in you getting visitors, or 'traffic', to your site. That can be easily done if you have a small advertising budget to get started with. Paid YouTube advertising is not the main topic of this book, but I do know a lot about it and I can share that information with you if you're interested in future books or courses that I create for you. But I will say this, right now, YouTube traffic and buying ads on YouTube is dirt cheap. And it's not hard to get a good campaign working if you know what you're doing. The good thing is, you're in great hands right now because this is what I do. And like I said, you don't need paid traffic to get started. It's a plus to ramp things up for yourself a lot faster though.

Check out my free trainings where I share with you more ways on how all of that works as well, especially with the organic searches. I do this step-by-step video training so it's very easy-peasy to copy and apply what I'm talking about here. I even show you how to create and launch your own digital products and sell them online. Get more information at: www.TonyRichie.com/bookbonus

Once you start building your audience and you're getting traffic over to your site, you could start testing different offers of what you're selling. You could create your product by using PDF files, audio files like MP3s, video files, and create simple little membership sites.

When I first started out, it was a little challenging to get a membership site up and running. You needed to have a developer, have some special software and the integration was a hassle. Nowadays with advanced technology, it's so much easier. Somebody with no technical skills at all can go in and create their own website or membership site. It's really easy; literally with the clicks of a few buttons and entering the name of your membership site you can have one created in an afternoon.

I am still a total tech dunce and I always was. I had to hire some web coders when I first started, subbing them out in India or even in the US, and nowadays, it's so easy. I manage all of my websites myself. I can show you exactly how to do this as well. If I can do it, you can do it. Once you have your technology set up, your membership site set up, and automatic delivery of your product, then you set up your buy buttons with your merchant account.

You'll be able to accept credit cards from customers all over the world by using merchant processors like Stripe, Braintree, or Paypal. How cool is that? Once that's set up, you can gauge and track to see your conversions and sales. I'll show you exactly how to do all of this.

After your initial setup of your systems, your main task will be to continue to put out awesome free content in the form of video at least once a week.

If you have a little budget, experiment and test with a little paid advertising. It doesn't have to be a lot. Five to ten dollars a day in paid ads just to get some people over to your site and seeing how many sales you make. This is it in a nut-shell.

Chapter 5

Launching Your Ultimate Lifestyle Business In 30 Days or Less!

Let's take this all a step further and get into the nitty-gritty... You need a step-by-step action plan so you know what steps you need to take to build your online business. So, let's get started.

The first step is to **identify** what market you want to get into. This usually starts off by discovering what you enjoy talking about, what you're already knowledgeable in, or by solving a problem that you currently have.

Example: You have bad credit, and you did a few months of research and you actually took the steps to repair your credit. You did it yourself and learned a ton in the process. Now you have first-hand experience and knowledge in credit repair. You can now teach others how to do the same! I know of somebody who actually did this without using YouTube and made millions of dollars selling a credit repair course. There is just so much opportunity out there right now. So, here's how you would do it by using YouTube...

You write a small book that detail the steps and resources that people need to clear their credit. You could even include a three to five video series to the course and package it up really nice. Awesome! You're now in the information marketing business. You're now selling your own digital or physical book online! "7 Proven Steps to Repairing Your Credit for FREE." Congratulations! I just made up that title by the way. If it's available and you're into credit, use it! That's a free title for you to use or improve on.

You can spend a day, or you can spend a week thinking this out.

Obviously the quicker you move on your idea, the quicker you move to the next step.

If you are confused right now, just try and figure out what your passion is... It can be something that you like talking about and would share with the world. If you don't, think about what you are interested in. Think about what you can talk about, what can you share, how you can add value to other people's lives by sharing what you know or by helping solve other people's problems...

Once you figure out what market you want to get into, you want to do a little further research on that topic so you start to become an expert on that topic.

We humans learn from others and we teach and share as our own. Sometimes we learn and we teach as is, without editing what we learned or without modifying what we learned.

Sometimes we learn something, then input our own strategies and experiences to create a totally new learning experience for somebody. Then we put that information out so somebody can take that strategy that's much simpler than it would be, without putting your ideas or tips in.

Once you start to educate yourself on your chosen topic, you'll see how easy it is to learn and teach new things, so buy a couple of books and have extra resources on the side so you have them for ideas. I did this same thing when I created my automotive courses. I bought a few automotive repair books to get a ton of ideas and even help in organizing my own courses. How cool is this!

The next thing you want to do is write up a small video **marketing and distribution plan**. Since we were just talking about credit repair, let's continue on that topic.

When I say you want to have a small video marketing plan, this is what I mean, and you can do this the exact same way for every other niche market out there.

Start by putting out good content on the internet in the form of videos. You can have your videos transcribed like I do and put them up on your website as a blog post to 5x its power because now you'll be benefiting from the content being on your site in text format, which will boost your search engine rankings. Yes, there is a little more work involved, but this is why you'll eventually sub this part out to your virtual assistant when you start getting things going. Again, this may sound intense, but when you stop thinking about it and just do it, you'll see that it's a piece of cake.

So not only do you have your video juice working for you, which has great content on it, you have your blog article, which has your keywords in it, and the Google search engine bot will crawl your website and see all of the related keywords in your article and give your site higher rankings. It's as simple as that.

Then, you want to commit to a frequent and timely upload strategy. When pushing content to the web or YouTube, you want to make sure you're on some sort of a schedule. Try to do a video a week and commit to it. Not only will it be good for your YouTube channel health, how they rank you and for your subscribers, but it will be good for you personally. You'll feel good about yourself that you're following a plan and that you're getting things accomplished.

Commit to one video a week when first starting, then see if you can to do two or three. If you can start with three, then more power to you!

If you decide that every Monday you're publishing a new video, commit to it. If you want to get even more specific and have better results, publish a video every Monday at 9am or 9pm, or whatever time you decide. The key is to be as consistent as you can with your video upload days and times. YouTube will see that you are a serious partner and give you better results and rankings over time.

Plus, you'll condition your audience and they'll know when to expect your new video. They'll expecting your new video like a mini TV show. I must admit, I personally don't commit to a certain time, but I do currently publish 2 videos a week to one of my YouTube accounts on set days. Every Monday and Thursday. My other account, I only publish one video a week, on every Wednesday. I am currently setting up my new channel, which I plan to get out at least 3 videos a week in the form of livestreams. Livestreams are very cool and are the newest part of the YouTube Live/Google Plus system. They just combined them and now if you want to go live you'll be using YouTube to do it.

I've been testing this feature out for the past few months and I've got to say, there fun as hell to do and you can sell your products and services while you're doing them live. I've created a 20-30 Minute show formula that you can copy. I will include a link to where you can learn more about this formula and get it on my site. I think you'll enjoy seeing how this is working like gangbusters for me. Get it at:

www.TonyRichie.com/bookbonus

So, this is essentially how you want to schedule your video uploads. Most times I do it like this, but sometimes I just can't because of my current lifestyle, and flying all over the world. Sometimes it gets a little tricky to manage but the point is, the more on time and on schedule you can be with your upload strategy, the better. Here's another trick that will help you get this down even better.

There is a feature in the backend settings of YouTube which you can use to schedule your video posts to be published. What you do is get things done in advanced. Take a day or two and just get in video creation mode. Make as many five to seven minute videos as you can. Let's say you made five videos and they are ready to go.

You can take those five videos, upload them, and you can set each one to be published every Monday night at eight o'clock PM, or two times a week. This allows you to have the flexibility to basically set your own upload schedule and have it happen on time, every week on its own, which is very nice. I've been personally using this feature a lot and have 4 months of video content preloaded and set to release once a week. It's a nice feeling when you have it all set to automate like that.

Once you have your videos, you can set them to release and it will automatically be published to your YouTube account and will look like fresh content for your audience each and every week. This will help you look and be consistent with your video publishing. It looks good to your subscribers and also, it's a plus for your YouTube channel health and rankings.

So that's number three. Get your content out and use an upload schedule. It's important if you want massive success with this, and it's really not a hard task at all.

Number four is to work on your **lead magnet.** Your free bribe, the promised material (could be a free cheat sheet, PDF, video) you offer to your lead (which is your website visitor) to get them to enter their name and email on your site. Let me give you a simple breakdown on how this looks. I call it the 'value ladder.'

An interested user visits your site, and in this case, we're talking credit repair, right? Still with me? Great. So the visitor visits your website (from your video that you had on YouTube) and the first thing they see is an offer that you've made to them to get a free 5-step credit assessment guide that will help them grade themselves on how bad, or how not bad they are with their credit. This step will help them get closer to their end goal (to repair their credit) because they would understand their own situation a lot better. Now for them to get this free credit assessment, they would need to enter their name and email on your webform to get it.

Now, that lead is in your email marketing funnel! Congratulations. They raised their hand and said, I need help with my credit and entered their name and email to get more information on your site. In this case, it was your 5-step credit assessment guide in which they would be able to grade themselves on where they actually stand. It can be a simple PDF guide they print out, or even an online survey style. Both are easy to setup and have completely automated working for you 24/7/365!

The *number one rule* to online marketing success is this: you always want to get someone's name and email information when they start hitting your website. You need to start and build an email marketing list as soon as possible. With the systems that I use, it's so simple to setup. I can help you get one up and running for yourself in an afternoon.

With that said, you can offer an immediate paid special offer with a discount when they get the free information from you, or you can hold off and sell them your complete booklet and training a few days down the line as you continuously market to them daily or every other day through your automated email marketing system. You'll soon see how this amazing world of automation works after you set this up. Again, it's not hard! It's pretty darn awesome if you ask me.

As you distribute all of your free content through YouTube, at the end of your content videos you're going to have a little call to action saying,

"Hey, thanks for watching my video. I hope you learned a lot. To learn more strategies, please click the link below. I'm giving away a free video series 'on this, or that' and you're not going to want to miss out!" Of course, you would edit this to match your persona, style and work in what you are actually offering. In *TubeCashSystem*, I show you the entire process and how to set all of this up very easily in the video members area so don't worry if this seems a bit dry. It's a little hard to get very detailed when talking about this over text. It's much easier showing you over videos, but I hope you get the point here.

You always want to give them, your viewer, a clear call to action at the end of every video that you make so they can click on it and go to your site. On your site, you'll have a headline that's congruent with your call to action. It can be a video explaining how to get the free bribe, or a text format headline. You can have a video saying, "Hey, thanks for coming here. All you have to do to get a free manual is put your name and email below. Click download and we will send you an automatic download link." Then, they can just download it and enjoy.

This is how you'll automatically build your leads. Also, in the same video, you're going to want to say, "Thanks for watching my video, if you liked it, please hit like and subscribe." Also, "Click the link below to get your free book." You want to remind them to subscribe. When they subscribe to your YouTube channel, you'll start building your audience which ends up being a beautiful thing.

So back to the funnel. You direct them to your website, you get their personal name and email information. Now, you can have them in your marketing funnel.

Let's do a little dreaming… Imagine having ten videos out there and they're sucking in three to five hundred video views a day and you're getting a hundred visitors to your website every day and twenty-five of them raise their hand and want more information by putting their name and email into your webform.

If you did those numbers, you'll be getting a 25% conversion and if you can do that, you're doing pretty darn good. If you're doing less than that, then you have room for some improvement. My team can help you do better.

You can optimize your lead page, and I'll show you strategies on how to do this and get at least a 25% conversion. If you're doing 50% - 60% conversion on your opt-in leads like I do on most of my sites, then you're doing excellent.

Now imagine you're getting five hundred visitors a day to your website, and you convert at an ok 30%. That's one hundred and fifty leads that are opting-in to your newsletter to get your free bribe. You're getting one hundred and fifty leads a day that are interested in what you do! They are interested in you; they are interested in your products and your services. Wow.

Once you have something like this working for you, can you imagine how big this can get? And you can market to these people, create a relationship and sell products automatically at the same time and it just gets bigger and bigger every single month.

Now, let's take it a step further and add in some sales because I really want to excite your imagination here. I mean, this was the stuff that got me excited when I first started out. I would think of these numbers and they got me excited and motivated to start doing things so I could see results.

Let's say that you get this thing up and humming and within 4-6 months you're generating 1,000 free video views a day, and this is not unrealistic by any means. And let's just say, out of those 1,000 views only 5% make it to your website to learn more. You may think, "what, only 5%?" From experience and making money by doing this for years, I will say that 5% is a conservative and pretty much accurate number.

Reason is, out of your 1,000 video views, some users may have just stumbled onto your video… others are just browsing, some not too serious and some very serious. So, you get 50 interested people heading over to your site in a day. That's actually not bad when you know they are targeted prospects. Let's say that you did your job and you're getting a solid 50% opt-in rate. This means that 50% of the people who visit your page will put in their email to learn more. You've got a solid 25 leads per day now, around 750 leads a month.

Let's say you do an ok job in selling your product to them via your automated email newsletter and you successfully sell them a $67.00 product. 3% buy the product. That gives you a solid 22.5 products sold each month. Let's do the math. $67.00 x 22.5 That gives you a total income of $1,507.50! Not too bad for getting started! And there are a lot of other ways to easily increase your income with the same number of leads and buyers that can literally double your income almost overnight. Imagine getting 100 leads per day with the same system. That my friend is a solid $6,000 plus per month!

Now, all you have to do to make more money is, 1. Get more video views which will result in more leads. You can add additional products to your funnel, and you can also test and increase conversions on your (free bribe page/lead page), your (sales page/your offer) and on.

And this is the FUN part. Once you have your system up and running, all you need to do is test new ideas and offers and make more money! And with the systems that we use today, it makes it so easy to do.

Next, get your free bribe done. Just because we set up our other steps before we created our actual free giveaway doesn't mean that we can't have them set up. I actually like to work this way because as people enter your system asking for more information, you have a chance to question them to see and figure out exactly what they're looking for, then you can go out and finish up, create and deliver what you promised on your free offer page that you set up in exchange for their email. Now is the time to get it done. Don't promise too much; make it something simple that you know you'll be able to create within a few days.

Now, at this point you've created your simple webpage and have your irresistible free offer setup.

The next step is to get a nice E-book cover graphic made up. It's always nice to have a graphic of what you're giving them so people can see that it's something of value. Just make it look really good. Of course, people know that it's just a download, but you want to show them a nice, sexy looking book. It motivates them to put in their name and email into your form. They want to get it because it looks cool.

If you want to do a video series, just have a nice screenshot of the YouTube video or a private video of you with some special secret that you'll be revealing.

You can also set it up where when people click on that video which is a dummy video, then a pop up appears and says, "Hey, put your name and email to unlock this video series." This is how you build your email list.

Once you start building your audience, and people are opting-in, they're liking what you do…. The next step is to basically sell your stuff. If you already have your product created, and you know what your market wants, then you can start positioning your offers, your emails and newsletters to start selling your program and you'll start making money!

I can show you how to create these simple little mini channels on YouTube where you'll build a cool little following and audience where you'll actually enjoy talking to them, helping them and at the same time automatically sell your products and services. Let me tell you that once you get one of these systems going, you'll see how rewarding it feels and how awesome it is because you can literally run this from anywhere on the world and generate a nice steady income from it.

Years ago, I started with an idea and I got into the automotive space on YouTube. I started putting videos out talking about cars. I was helping people with cars, teaching them how to buy or, how to sell them, how to repair certain things on them, and sooner than later, I started gathering a large audience.

In about four to six months, people started subscribing to my channel, they started to message me asking me where they can learn more and asking if I had more to offer. At that time, I was just directing people to other websites because I didn't have anything yet of my own to sell them. I was sending them to my competitors' sites, believe it or not.

Once you start building an audience on YouTube, they'll start to subscribe to you and your channel. Four months later, you might end up with five hundred leads in your mailing list. You can easily send them an email saying, "Hey, I'm in the process of creating this amazing product that's going to help you with your golf swing (assuming that you're a personal golf trainer or something) ... What is your burning question about golf? What is the most frustrating thing right now with your golf swing? I'm creating a product. How can I help you?"

You can ask them what their burning questions are pertaining to your niche. You're going to get a lot of replies. Out of five hundred, you'll probably get 15% replies or even more. Imagine 75 replies from an audience that's interested in your stuff, interested to learn more, you can go back and forth a few times and create a super-duper information product for them.

That's how I did it. You create what they want. You figure out what their needs are, what they're looking for and what they need help with, and then you create a product from all of that market feedback.

It's a great learning process, too, because you'll be able to learn so much more about your audience than you would have never known by not communicating to them.

It's very important to communicate with your audience. You'll get to know them a lot better which will allow you to be a better marketer. You'll be able to put out better content on YouTube, on video, you'll get people more interested because that's what they're searching for. They're searching for these keywords that you've dialed in and are talking directly to them.

That's how you do it. Then, you create a product. Once you've created a product, then you can start selling and monetizing all your efforts 24/7/365. You create a product once you go through this process.

The next step is designing and creating your **funnel**.

This is very easy to do right now with all the technology that we have. You don't have to be a computer tech. I'm still a one-finger typist computer dunce till this day. I am not techie at all.

But, once you know these strategies, you can continuously create products that sell, help other people and grow your online business at the same time. I still get thank you emails every day from my email subscribers and customers every single day. And some of them are really nice to read.

Just like that, you're set. You have no boss to worry about. It's such a gratifying feeling when you have a system like this running for you. You have all this traffic coming to your websites and your only job after that, and I wouldn't even say that it's a job, but your only task is to continue to put out good content and test your funnels to see what makes more sales for you.

In this last phase, your focus would be getting more traffic and coming up with more marketing strategies, creating more products to sell, and testing new ideas to get more reach. That's the game. And of course, you will be learning a ton more as you go. The main things are to get your topic down and make your first video! That's it!

Focus, Time Management and Getting Things Done

Focus and time management is a crucial part to getting things accomplished, getting goals accomplished and pumping out important things to move your business and your life forward.

Every day we have choices to make. Every day and every minute, we can either procrastinate, push it aside or take action and get things done.

Everybody has this devil of procrastination on their shoulders. We're always looking for an easy way out and as you know water travels the path of least resistance. With humans, it's an innate form of nature with us. We want to take the easy path.

We have to force ourselves to actually get the important things done in order to accomplish the big things in life. So I will say this - make it a point to set some goals for yourself and act upon them daily. If your goal is to create your first YouTube channel after reading this book, do it. Get started. Open a free account, then go about learning how to correctly set it up so you can start adding your fun and awesome content videos. And before you know it, people will start watching your videos, subscribing, and you'll be on your way to building your very own audience, and then your own money making online business. To succeed online, you need an audience.

You need traffic (viewers and visitors) and you need to have a simple product to sell. And in my advanced but easy to follow training system, I show you exactly how to get this all up and running, working 24 hours, 7 days a week, 365 days a year for you, the right way. Be sure to head over to **www.TonyRichie.com/bookbonus** to see how this can work for you, even if you're just getting started.

Imagine having your very own international internet business that you can run from anywhere in the world. How cool is that? Well, I've been doing this for years and I do not make the bulk of my money teaching this stuff. I do this in other markets and do very well. The good thing for you is that you're dealing with a true, in the trenches marketer and teacher. Everything that I learn, I test and apply to my own business, I then share my results and what's working best for me with you. You will always be on the cutting edge of what's working now. I look forward to seeing you inside of the VIP member's area if you decide to join us. Moving on.

Chapter 6

No Experience, No Problem.
Formulate Your USP and Get People
To Buy From You Now!

I'm starting this chapter bluntly. It will be extraordinarily difficult to succeed if you don't have a product and persona that sets you apart from the rest of the pack. The good news is, most people don't know how to do this nor do they know how to pull it off. The better news for you is, it's not hard to accomplish. You just need to create your Unique Selling Proposition (USP) and you can do this by completing a few steps and by thinking it out.

The unique value that you offer and deliver to your customers, compared to your competitors, is referred to as your Unique Selling Proposition (USP), also called your Unique Value Proposition. Why should someone buy from you versus anyone else? What extra value can you offer? How can you position yourself differently? Look closely at what you want to offer people as part of your business model. Then, you'll need to answer the following questions from the very start of your online business:

1. What are you offering?
Lay out the details of the product or service you plan to sell. What are the features? What does it do for them? What does it look like? For example, is it a 14-day mini e-course on how to catch fresh water bass? Is it a 6-month coaching program that gives people direct access via email or phone to you personally? Be very specific.

2. How does it solve customers' problems?
How does your product offering solve your customers' problems? State the problems your customer is facing, which you should know from doing your market research. Then describe how each feature of your

product or service solves those problems. Think about how your customer would see your solution, not knowing you at all. If you can answer the question "What's in it for me?" from the customer's viewpoint, you're already halfway there.

3. What is different about it?

You must create a product or service that is distinct from your competitors. While it is possible to be successful by creating a "me-too" site, it will be far, far more difficult in the long run. How is your solution different from other people? Are you offering something extra, such as training or additional services? Do you offer your product in multiple formats, such as audio and video? Do you provide extra tools to make your solution easier to use? If you can't identify any features that are different about your product, now is the time to go back and create something.

4. Why should someone buy from you vs. your competitors?

This is by far the toughest part of creating your USP. It will also be one of the most important parts of your sales copy. Tie together the problems your potential customers are facing, the features of your product, and how they solve your prospects' problems. Then pull in your extra "proof" of why people should buy from you. You could have social proof through testimonials of how well your solution works. You might have a track record of experience in your industry. You could also have great examples of your solution in action. Which of these are most important to your market? Pick one or use them all depending on what you think your prospects need to hear. Give them what they want.

If you have already done extensive market research, then you know what problems your customers are facing. Make sure you thoroughly understand what your target customers want and what your competitors are already offering. Then you will be able to identify exactly what you can do differently or where you can add something more. Put all of that together and you have your Unique Selling Proposition.

Attraction Marketing

In this chapter, we're going to talk about the attraction marketing strategy. We're going to develop sales messages that magnetically attract the perfect costumers. You will discover the easiest and quickest way to motivate the right type of prospect to your business, how to create a persuasive and compelling marketing message to your target audience, and how to make your business stand head and shoulders above your competitors.

I'm going to give you a list that you can use to make your products or service the clear and obvious choice to your ideal customer. And, last but not least, you're going to discover the truth about the secret way to break through to skeptical prospects and to have them block them into your business to purchase from you.

Answer This Question

Why should a prospect choose you or your product/service over any and every other option that's available to them, including doing nothing? See, the reality is, if you can't answer that question, then it's time to go back to the basics and start all over again. You must be able to answer the question about why a prospect should choose you over any other option, over any other options that they have, including doing nothing. This is also known as you're Unique Selling Proposition or USP. Some places call it the extra value proposition or even the competitive advantage.

But, regardless of the name that you call it, you must have an answer for that all-important question. I hear some of the worst and absolutely weakest USP's. I know business owners who say they been in business X amount of years and things like the lowest price guarantee, or we sell everything, or even satisfaction guaranteed.

Those things don't resonate with the market place. Every business can say, 'We've been in business a certain amount of years.' Every business can say, 'Oh, we guarantee the lowest prices,' or 'We sell everything. Your satisfaction guaranteed.' Those things do not connect with the specific type of customer that every business ownership should be going at.

How Do Other Companies Do It?

Here are some examples of unique selling propositions, or USP's that really sell. For example, Fed-Ex said 'When it absolutely, positively has to be there the next day.' Think about that for a second. We know that if it had to be there tomorrow, we had to use Fed-Ex. No other mail service carrier could provide that service. Things have changed now, but obviously back then, that was the truth, and we all knew it.

What about Re-Max. They guarantee that 'they'll sell your house in 90 days or they'll sell it for free.' So, if you're a home owner and you need to move quickly or you have a job promotion relocating you and you needed to sell your home quickly, they guarantee that they will sell your home in 90 days or you won't have to pay them to sell it. That's pretty powerful.

What about Domino's? Their USP was 'delivery in 30 minutes or it's free.' Very powerful. So, if you were hungry and you needed a pizza fast, then you chose Domino's.

These are some examples of USP's that really sell. See, that USP or Unique Selling Proposition that connects with your market place can make a huge difference.

Raymour and Flanigan, a furniture company in the New England area, guaranteed delivery of your furniture in three days or less. Every other furniture company was making their customers wait two and three weeks. But, Raymour and Flanigan were able to do it in three days or less. Their USP allowed them to capture a huge amount of the market place by offering a USP that connected with their target market, that customers were willing to pay a premium for.

What do all those USP's have in common? Well, they're in high competition industries and businesses.

So, if you're tempted to use that as your excuse by saying your industry is too competitive, then look to the previous companies for examples. These are examples of companies that are in high competition industries and they took USP's that spoke to their target market. In fact, most target a niche within a niche. So, with the example of Domino's, not everyone likes the taste of Domino's pizza, but if you need a quick pizza and you need it right away because you have a hungry family or friends stopped by, you knew you had to choose Domino's.

When choosing Fed-Ex as a customer, you may not agree with Fed-Ex's pricing, but because you need your documents delivered to a destination the next day, you choose them. The same is also true for Raymour and Flanigan, because while everybody doesn't need their furniture in three days, many customers do and are willing to pay a premium for quicker delivery.

All of those examples that I just gave you share the fact that all three companies sell regular boring products or services. If they did it, so can you. But, you have to take the time to put it together. So, what I am going to reveal to you is five proven USP's strategies that you can use in your business without lowering your prices. The other things that the example companies also have in common is that most of them charge a premium.

They are not the lowest price leaders in their niches. They may charge a premium. So, while there may have been many pizza restaurants who charged less at that point in time that Domino's, those other restaurants would not guarantee delivery in 30 minutes or less.

How To Get Customers To Happily Pay Your Higher Prices And Fees

Here are USP's strategies that you can use in your business to give you some ideas that you can implement without lowering your prices. After all, this marketing and business-building program is about doubling and increasing your profits. It's not about carving a way and reducing your profits.

USP Strategy #1

The first USP strategy you could use is product packaging. You can have a unique product or package that your competitor doesn't have. An example of this would be products by Apple or the George Foreman Grill. There are lots of PC's or laptops available in the market place. But, Apple has done something very special in the way that they create their product, the way they put it together; their whole packaging, their image, their marketing.

Secondly, look at the George Foreman Grill. It's just a grill, a little counter top grill, but their package has a unique angle because of their spokesman. So, those are examples of the product being unique or the packaging being unique. Now, you could always bundle up several products and services and call that bundle unique.

This is usually the most difficult USP to create because you must have the ability to literally change the product or package. So, once again, this first USP strategy is about creating a unique product. So, if you don't have the ability to create a product from beginning, then this may not be the best USP option for you. However, you can put together several different products or get several different services.

For example, let's say you're a pharmacy. You could put together a traveler's kit comprised of several different products by several different vendors or suppliers. You could bundle it and sell it for a much higher price than the individual prices of each component.

Restaurants are really good at doing this. However, you can still do this even if you're offering services. So, even if you were just a plumber or an electrician, you could package several different services and call this a 'home owner's deluxe' or something similar, where you do the kitchen, the bathroom, check the outside, etc. You can do all these things, but you have to think outside the box a little bit.

USP Strategy #2

The second USP strategy can be based on something unique about the way the product is constructed or about the way the customers help. An example of this would be a car repair shop, like Monroe Mufflers, who walks every customer through a customized 32-point check-up.

This can be easily applied to many industries such as the real estate industry by loan officers and mortgage brokers, who could walk their clients through this 24-point check list of what they need to do before they buy a home. This can work for dentists or lawyers or any service base business.

For example, if your name was Mike Brown, you could say, 'Mike Brown's Deluxe Customization.' Something where you could put the name together and 'Mike Brown's 24-point Checklist.'

USP Strategy #3

The third strategy is based on the business owner's personality or persona by putting a face on the advertising in marketing that connects with their target market. An example of this would be the gecko by Geico or the duck mascot by Affleck. You can see a lot of local places that will also get local celebrities, whether it be a local sport star, or local celebrity enterprise on radio or television.

On a smaller scale, this could be a local business owner starring in his/her own television commercial. There have been a lot of examples over the years of local business owners who became the first valuable persona of their business. That's a very effective strategy that's been proven to work.

In my opinion, every small business owner should be the face of their company, with rare exceptions. Generally speaking, you want to make a person to person connection. It's a much stronger bond, which is why Hollywood celebrities are paid so much more for providing entertainment. That's what the goal of the local business owner should be, especially in service base businesses, where you're working one on one with the client. You want them to feel that they know you when they walk into your office or walk in an appointment or meeting with you.

USP Strategy #4

The fourth USP strategy is based on providing a very unique or high level of service. A good example of this is the 'W Hotel' offering a whatever-whenever service, that delivers exactly what it promises.

So, you have to come up with a way to offer a higher level of service and unique products that you can offer for premium pricing. Many business owners will argue with this, but think about it for a minute. If everyone was just concerned about buying the lowest price, then no one would ever buy a Mercedes, or Lexus, or Bentley. If customers are only concerned about the lowest price, all these high-end retailers would go out of business.

There are high-end retailers and businesses that are struggling because they don't have great levels of service after they charged a premium, but for the most part, there's a marketplace for every price point. You just have to figure out how to create your high level, high premium product and service for premium price in your niche, in your industry, in your business.

This could be a 24/7 or in-home level of service. For example, there are many people who would never want to manage a rehab project. They would pay a premium in a higher level of pricing for the ability to have someone do it for them, and just send them a weekly report, or send them a daily update, etc. You have to begin to think along those lines. I believe every business owner should have a top, high level quality product or unique service that they offer for a higher price.

USP Strategy #5

The fifth USP strategy is based on a unique marketing strategy or technique. It's doing a unique way of advertising. For example, Red Bull designed cars with a red can on top to drive around giving free samples to college students across the world. It was a worldwide global campaign that was a very unique way of marketing their company and it worked very well.

There are dozens of ways to have unique messaging. Another example is zip cars, which are cars that you can rent for short trips, such as running errands for a couple of hours. However, their cars are a traveling billboard for their business because every car has the zip car logo and website on it.

Using this strategy can separate you from the competitors in the mind of your market place. The goal is to find a unique marketing strategy or tactic that no one else is doing. So, for example, if everyone in your industry is only doing direct mail, maybe you can continue to do direct mail but you might move into a new area where you're now doing a video conference or online marketing that's creative.

You want to do something unique. So, if you're doing what everyone else is doing, that's not unique. You want to look at your market, and then you want to try to find an effective way that is different than everyone else is doing to market your message, but still is effective.

The Key To A Powerful USP

The key to a powerful USP is to make sure that it is precise enough to echo the prospect's thoughts. For example, let's say I owned a mattress store and I wanted to sell high level premium mattresses for morbidly obese individuals. So, on my advertising, my USP would be, "Our mattresses are built so well, you can literally drive a truck over them and then sleep on them." I could drive a truck over my mattress to illustrate the point or leave a bulldozer on my mattresses overnight and see how well they spring back to their original shape in the morning. Those are just a few examples off the top of my head. At the end of the day, you want to make sure your USP is that specific, so it echoes the prospects own thoughts.

Also, you want to make sure your USP addresses the biggest objection that a prospect would have to buying your product or service. Let's say, for example, you were an insurance agent. You want to know that most people's biggest objections or fear of buying insurance is maybe talking about death, or maybe talking about the accident that could happen to trigger that. So, you want to make sure that USP addresses that.

Let's say you're targeting the person who's doing the shopping for a mattress and has tried four or five different mattresses. They've tried the cheap ones, they've tried the firm ones, they've tried the high ones, but they're not just built for heavy individuals. As a business owner of a mattress shop, when you do your marketing campaign you want to make sure that you're USP promises to solve all of the prospect's problems related to purchasing your mattress. That's where good product or service guarantees come in to place. So, the mattress shop owner could say, "We guarantee that your mattress will support your blah, blah, or money back", or something to the effect we will replace it.

Make Them Laugh or Cry

Next, your USP has to include the dominant emotion. For example, you want to know why they would buy a product or service that you offer. For example, let's revisit buying insurance. Why does a prospect buy insurance? They're buying it because they want to protect their family. It doesn't matter if you target the husband, wife, parents or children. You want to make sure that you talk about the one thing they're feeling.

As a husband, it may be making sure that his wife is taken care of in case anything happens to him while at work or traveling. He knows that taking good care of his family would ease the burden on his wife. He might be thinking about the fact that his wife will have to go and work three jobs to support the family. You want to include that dominant emotion in the USP. And then you want it to be unique enough to be easily remembered.

Creating A Good USP Is Hard Work

Now, I do realize that developing a good USP is hard work, but a good USP can make the difference between struggling to meet payroll and having the best year ever. But here's the catch. No matter how good your USP is, you must be able to consistently deliver on your promise or you're better off not having a USP at all.

Once again, no matter how good your USP is, you must be able to consistently deliver your promise or you're better off not having a USP at all. You must give a customer a compelling reason to buy from your business. So, no matter how great you think your product or company is, if you don't have a compelling USP, then you are just another faceless company in a long list of faceless companies.

So, you may personally think that your widget or services are the best, but if you have no way to communicate that to your target market, and to the prospects consistently in a persuasive and compelling way, then you're just essentially invisible.

You Know Your USP Is Good When...

You know your USP is good when the costumers come in and say the only reason that they came in is because of your USP, not because of your super low prices.

You don't want to attract customers to your business by constantly lowering your lowest prices. You want them to come in because your USP spoke to them. You want your USP to target their direct situation and cause them to take action.

Also, you know your USP is good when a prospect drives by your competitor's business, parks their car in your competitor's parking lot because yours is too crowded on that weekend, just to walk across the street and buy from you, because you're the expert.

The best part about great USP's is that they allow you to charge premium prices and earn massive profits selling the products or services that your customers love and feel good about buying.

It's in your best interest to turn your business into an industry leader that's known for being the go-to expert because expert's can get away with charging more.

How Many USP's Do You Need?

You can have more than one USP. So, you may have a campaign that focuses on one specific USP, because you're targeting one specific market place. For example, if you are a real estate agent, you could target one neighborhood and say, "You guarantee the sale of the house in this neighborhood in 90 days or less or you sell it for free." In fact, it's smart to develop a USP for each target market you're going up against.

It's even better if you can create a separate plan for each target market, but that's not always possible. But, you definitely want to make sure there's clear separation. Be crystal clear about what you're offering for each USP, what product and services you are offering and exactly what's going on with each offer.

Why Do Business Owner's Hate To Use USP's?

If an effective USP is so powerful, then why do most company and business owners not do it? Because, it takes real work and it's dramatically different than what they're doing now.

See, the things and step in the process that I just shared with you is going to take some time. It's going to mean that you're going to have to create some offer, spend a couple of hours talking to your customers and put some examples together. It takes real work.

Next, many business owners are just too lazy and too comfortable to do the work. Many other business owners refuse to develop new products. They don't even want to develop new marketing strategies, different sales techniques or anything else that takes work.

Lastly, some business owners are just too stubborn. They refuse to listen to customers, staff, the market, legislations, etc. So, the point of it all is that creating an effective USP does take work. There's no way around it.

You can't rely on guessing. You have to go out and get real answers to these very real problems that you're facing in your business. And, once you develop a USP, put your USP everywhere. Put it on your business card, your voice mail, your business signs, your phone greetings, your letter heads, your stationary, sales receipts and websites because you want everyone to know you for what you do very, very well.

So in conclusion, you must develop a USP that connects with your target market and gives them a compelling reason to do business with you. Next, an effective USP allows you to charge premium prices while creating a database of clients and customers who will love your company.

Yes, USP's take work, but the advantages are tremendous. It will make a huge impact on your bottom line. You could have more than one USP. As a matter of fact, I advise you to have more than one USP. As soon as you develop one that works, develop a second one for another target market. Put your USP everywhere in your business. Finally, you want to do well, and you want to make sure that your market place and your target market knows exactly who you are and what you are selling.

Chapter 7

Content Is Queen... Distribution is King!

As you get into the information marketing business, you will hear many people say that content is king. And I do believe content is important. However, I realized (though years of research and learning) that distribution is even more important than content.

Think about this. If nobody sees what you have to offer, what good is it? If you can't get what you're selling and offering out to the world to see, how do you expect to make any sort of impact? You need to be and get seen to be effective in this world. The world revolves around people buying, and people selling. Sell or be sold. You may have heard me say this before but once I was reading this book by Robert Kiyosaki and it stuck with me. That quote burned into my brain. He said, "If you want to become rich, you need to sell things" You need to sell other people's stuff, your stuff, whatever. It doesn't matter, but you need to sell. And if you think you can't sell, get over it. Stop thinking like a baby. Learn to sell, just like I did. This is a learned skill and anybody can learn to become a better and more effective seller to build and grow their empire.

In chapter 5 we talked about creating wonderful content. In creating content, the first thing to do is to have a finished finalized video and upload it to your YouTube channel. What is finish finalized video? A finished finalized video is a 5- to 7-min content video edited into a computer using a quick, easy-editing software like iMovie or Camtasia or similar other editing software, added with a quick little intro and outro.

This will not seem to be too technical even if you're a complete novice to the computer. It's very easy. I'm not a technical guy myself, so I don't do crazy video editing and you don't have to be a video editing pro to get good stuff out and get people to like your videos. Just do simple edits, add a little intro and outro and a few other tricks. I have a complete training series that will take you step-by-step through this entire process so you can build out your new business online fast. It's not as hard as it may sound. It can seem this way because most of what you're seeing here are words on paper. Not a video saying, do this, do that, or click here and there.

Let's just say that we've created your first video together. Now we can take a little image of the video, an eye-catching image with some text overlay of the headline, so if the video you made is talking about fishing and proper pole techniques, we'll take a catchy image from the video of you with the pole and slap a headline on it. This way you have a catchy video thumbnail that entices people to click on it.

As for your video intro, you could put in simple background music for around 5 seconds with your logo and then it will transition to the content part of the video, a very simple intro like that, then you can get into the meat of the content. You could even do a video headline style of intro. There are a few different kinds and are not set in stone.

The outro, on the other hand, is your call to action. It can be a combination of you saying a few things — and links to subscribe to YouTube. You can also have a text overlay in the ending of your video that says, "Click here to subscribe." You could easily put a button in the video editor, a button that people can click, and you will also have a little graphic of your website's logo, where people can click and go to your website as well. It's a simple image file that you can put right into your video editor and create a little mini outro.

You can add some music to it if you want. At the end of your video, basically from within YouTube, people could click that little link to subscribe to your channel, go to your website, or go watch your other videos, which is what you want. There are a couple of ways in doing this and we'll explain everything in my advanced step-by-step training that you can learn more about at: **www.TonyRichie.com/bookbonus**. The bottom line is, at the end of your video you want to integrate a "call to action" so the user knows what to do next. You guide them to like your video and visit your site to learn more. This is how you get visitors and targeted traffic to your website. This is what's needed to make money online :) Pretty simple, huh?

Alright, so let's say that we have your completed video ready-to-go. The next thing to do is upload our main video file to YouTube so people can start watching, enjoying, learning, and liking the video. What you also want to do with that file is to save a copy to your hard drive.

There are many different ways to back up your videos. I recommend at least two different places - one locally using your external hard drive and then one in the cloud somewhere or on another server that you have. Other examples are the Google Drive and Dropbox. The other kind of backup that you can do is to create a clone YouTube channel and just upload and store your videos there.

If you have a channel on YouTube that teaches people how to go fishing, and you're building an audience and subscriber base, you're 100% free to create a spinoff and rename the channel something else; just upload not the same exact video but maybe a shorter version of it, so it's not 100% alike. You need to do this because YouTube has its algorithms that basically try to prevent clone copies of your video.

So, it's good not to put in an exact clone copy. You want to at least take out 5 to 10 seconds of your video. When these algorithms run through it, the new video is not the exact file, and not of the same file size. The headline must also be renamed. Just change the headline; change a word or two. Now you have a second YouTube channel account with basically the same video up there. Just name it a little bit different. You could also put a longer or shorter intro and outro on the videos. Doing this leaves the content the same, but the end video file changes size. I do this as well, so I have a completely different account.

Why should you do this? I do this because I lost a YouTube channel once before, and it's always good to have a backup. Whatever the case was, once you got three strikes on your YouTube account with people complaining about the content, they can close your YouTube account down, and it only happened to me once. That channel that was shut down had about a hundred videos on it. Because I had a copy of everything, I was able to bounce back within six months and gain my full audience back plus some. All I did was have my virtual assistant (VA) consistently upload three videos every week until I got all my videos back on YouTube. It did take a few months to gain momentum and for people to start viewing my videos because it was a brand-new channel. But after six months, it started getting ground, I started getting a lot of traffic back to my website, and after a year, it was like I never lost anything. The good thing was that it wasn't my only channel.

Imagine if I didn't have a copy of any of those content videos. I would be going crazy, recreating everything again; you probably won't even do it. You'd probably just give up. So, it's always good to keep a copy of all your files. It may sound a little bit extreme, but remember we're talking about protecting a million-dollar business. It's worth it to keep a copy of your videos. It's insurance. If you're looking at making money online, your online assets are your business. It's everything, so you want to make sure to protect all of it.

For my paid membership sites that members pay for, it is a more advanced program and set of courses than my free stuff that I put online. You may ask where I host those videos to protect them. I don't put them on Facebook or YouTube. I put them somewhere where I can control 100% of it. There are a few services that you can subscribe to get premium video hosting plans instead of putting all of your premium content membership videos on YouTube. For some reason, if YouTube closes your account and you had your private member only videos hosted there, all of your members will lose access to all of those videos.

To host my videos, I use a software called EVS, or Easy Video Suite. It's hooked up to your own Amazon S3 account, and once you have that account, you could upload your videos to it and it will stream all your videos. Of course, you have to pay for it, but for a very small cost, maybe ten dollars a month, depending on how many videos you have. I have hundreds myself, so it's probably around $50-$70 dollars a month. That's the reason why I use Easy Video Suite. Here, you just drag your video and put it into that little app from your computer, then it uploads it right into your Amazon account, and you can just grab the link and put it in your membership site. In my case, my Amazon account is a secondary place where I back up my videos as well. And don't worry if you are curious on how all of this works; I show you how easy it is to setup. There are also other easy options. This is not the hard stuff.

On one membership site that I manage, I have close to four thousand paid members, and we're not going to say that all of them are on watching all the time. You only need a few paid members to pay for your sixty-dollar video hosting. A sixty-dollar month bill is nothing compared to what's coming in from membership fees every month. Bottom line is, hosting is a little cost compared to what you'll be making with your site.

Moving forward. We have created the videos, have a backup, have our videos protected and ready to upload them to YouTube. Let's talk about the process of getting started on YouTube. In order to have a YouTube account, all you need is a Google account. And now with Google, everything is integrated. You've got your Gmail account, you've got YouTube connected, you've got Google+ that can be connected, you've got Google Drive, you've got Google Docs, and you got all these Google apps that are connected to one account.

To get an account, you basically need one email address. So, to get started with YouTube, go to www.gmail.com; if you don't have a Gmail address, you create one. Create your free email address just like you would a Hotmail or yahoo email address. You've got to create a Gmail address. Once you have that, you have access to all of Google's apps using one email. Once you have your email address, you'll have your YouTube account as well. Just a tip: I would recommend that you use a professional sounding email address when you sign up for a Gmail account because people are going to see that. I usually do mine with my website name. So if I have fishinglikeapro.com, then my Gmail address would be fishinglikeapro@gmail.com or something close to the website name. This way it's all related.

Now you have all those accounts created. It's actually one account, but you can access all of the google app features, and when we say apps, we mean the different software's that you could use within Google: Gmail, YouTube, Google Drive, and so on.

Since you have your YouTube video created, all you have to do is go and log in to YouTube, and there's a little button on the top right-hand corner that says "Upload." You just click that button and pick the video out of your folders or wherever it's located in your computer and upload it. Another way is by dragging and dropping the video from your screen into the upload area. Once you do that, your video automatically starts uploading.

The next thing you do is to create your headline. There is a little headline area where you put your video headline in; you do want to make sure that you put in a catchy headline, so that when people see it, they are driven to click on it. Do the same thing in the description. Write a clear, at least one to two-paragraph description about the video: what people are going learn from the video and it should always be above the fold within the first or second sentence; you also include the URL to your website so people can visit your site to learn more and you can get them in as a lead to your funnel.

You want to make sure your website link shows up right in the description below your video without people having to scroll down. This is a big pointer not many take advantage of. There is also a certain way you want to spell out your link so it becomes clickable. If you just type in www.yourdomain, it will not be clickable to the viewer. They won't be able to just click it and visit your website. You want to make sure it looks like: http://www.yourdomain.com. Then it becomes a clickable link that drives them to your site.

You want to make sure that your URL is at the top sentence of your description, so that people can click it right away. When they're watching your video on YouTube, they're going to hear you say, "To get more information to get this free book, click the link below the video in the description box."

They will look down and see the URL, right there. This is an easy way for them to learn more from you and do business with you. That's the whole point of everything. You want it to be easy for them to look down and click and not have to open the dropdown box and go searching for the link that they need to click.

Next, you also have to enter in your tags, and your keywords for your video so it can be searched and seen by people. If you made a video on real estate, because you're an expert and have some tips and knowledge to share, you have to put in all the keywords relating to real estate that pertain to your video. This will help people find your video!

Originally when I was starting out, I researched other videos to see what the most popular searched terms (tags or keywords) were in my niche.

These tags are words unseen by people, but when they search using those keywords, it would bring the video that had those tags and keywords up. This is called keyword tagging. YouTube knows what your video is about, and these keywords help searchers find your video. Obviously, you're going to do a little bit of a keyword research and find out about what are the most searched keywords in your market. I show you exactly how to do this within the advanced courses that I offer to help you get started quicker. It's much easier showing you how to do this on video rather than talking about it here.

After creating a real, catchy headline title for your video, and you really want to get the competitive edge, have your virtual assistant (VA) transcribe your video and turn it into a readable article. This is what I started doing a few years after I got into this and I noticed a huge bump in video views.

As soon as the video is done and live on YouTube, I would grab the link and send it over to my VA and say, "Hey, please transcribe this for me." She would transcribe the whole video and make it blog-ready. She even posted it on my blog as a post and embedded the video above the article. If you are totally new to this, it may seem like a lot of work and over your head, but it's really not once you start following a system. It's a matter of getting one piece at a time done. Before you know it, it's a full content video, links to your site, and a readable article on your site. And it all is designed to deliver value, gain views and sell your stuff!

I used to do all of this myself. But nowadays, it's not necessarily what I do. My virtual assistants do it for me, for a minimal cost. I can show you where to hire help for as little as $1.50-$2.50 an hour! I mean, it's worth paying 4 dollars to have the whole thing transcribed and done for you because it will give you many more views and it will optimize your video and website.

I can't do it on my own now with the many videos that I upload every week. These transcripts can help you. They act like a lead magnet. You've got great content about your niche and you want to make sure you put this in many places as you can to make yourself as searchable as possible.

It helps a lot if you have a regular WordPress site or a Weebly blog where you can post your content besides just doing YouTube. Within the past two years, I've seen my organic search from Google just go up like crazy; a few years ago it was down, but now it started to come back a lot more, because of all the good quality content that Google finds on my site.

After that, if you have an email list or audience, then you want to make sure you send them a link to watch your new video as soon as you get it uploaded and it's ready for viewing. Getting views to your newly uploaded videos are important. I really stress to share it through as many distribution channels that you have laying around. If you have a Facebook following, Twitter, Instagram, whatever, you want to share that link to get views. Of course, if you have some YouTube subscribes at this point they will automatically get a notification from YouTube that you've uploaded a new video. And that's a good thing.

If you also did what I said, had your own website and started offering free stuff to build your email list, then you would send them an email saying that you've uploaded a new video for them. I do this for every video that I upload and it's fantastic. The cool thing when you have a list is that when you send them that update email talking about your new video, you can also send them a special offer to check out your paid stuff. And I bet you'll get some buyers :)

There are a couple of advanced things that we can get into and I cover it all out on video within the main course if you decide to let me help you build your online business. There are annotations and cards that you can use to increase interaction on your videos that get people to visit your site as well and they are ultra-powerful.

To sum this chapter up, this is what it looks like to get a killer video out that will get you thousands of views:

Create a content video, edit lightly using video editing software

Create a backup

Create a Gmail account or address

Sign in to your YouTube account

Upload your video (type in the headline, create thumbnail, description)

In my resource page, there is a checklist for you to copy and download. It will help you from forgetting some of these easy-to-do things that make a huge difference in the long run.

Chapter 8

The Evergreen Content Machine: Autopilot Fresh Leads and Customers for You 24/7

Let's say you did some work and got 10 videos uploaded onto YouTube. Each video that you uploaded addresses a main question that the market has. This will start to drive a lot of people to watch your videos if you do it right and just talk to your market. Many people out there don't create a dialogue with their audiences. Listen to them, and create videos that answer their questions. If you keep doing this, you'll soon hit the pot of gold. A lot of marketers are too lazy to continue to create content. This is an easy way to keep the content going for your tribe.

In your video, make sure that you weaved in your basic intro who you are, what you are going to talk about, what problems will be solved or talked about, and at the end of your video you have your call to action for them to learn more. The whole goal is to move the viewer to like your video, subscribe, then head over to your website to learn more. This is where you will present your offer in exchange for their name and email address.

You'll be giving them something in exchange for their email. It can be your seven-day video series on your website, a free report, an infographic, a cheat sheet, or whatever you decide to create and deliver to them.

Whatever you create, it needs a sexy title to get them really interested. Then you tell them, "don't forget, after watching this video click the link below" because in your YouTube description you're going to have your clickable website link that takes them directly to your website landing page so you can collect them as a lead!

For the few of you that don't know, a landing page is a simple one-page webpage that has a headline, a nice little infographic or a graphic of what you're going to give them in exchange for their name and email, and a couple of benefit driven bullet points. You could test with name and email or by just asking for their email. They say the fewer fields you have, the higher a conversion you will get. Which means, if you're asking for a name and email, that's two fields, versus just asking for their email address, which is one field. You can set up your thank you page and your autoresponder, which we're going to talk about in a few minutes, which will automatically send them whatever your free bribe was that you offered in the video.

But before we get into that, I want to stay with YouTube a little bit more. You have three ways to link people over to your website. The first one is in the description box, which is below the video, below the share buttons. There's a comment area and right above there you can put in your website URL and description. There's also something called annotations.

If you've ever seen those videos on YouTube, where there's a little box that you can click and has some text overlay, that's an annotation. Once you verify your website with YouTube and Google, they allow your users to virtually click that link, and it'll take them straight over to your website from within the video. That's an amazing feature, because your video could be embedded on any other website out there, and if people click, it goes straight to your website! That's super big.

There's also something new called YouTube cards, which is the same thing, but you could put a graphic of what you're offering in that card and it's viewable on mobile, and with the trends today only more and more people are going mobile. So it's business friendly. Now you've got it very easy for people who are interested in your stuff to get to your website from watching your video, which is pretty amazing!

My home study course will give you actual videos that will walk you through each step of this and how to apply. And most importantly, how to do it effectively as possible.

Now that the customer has gone to your website and has given you their email address, and received their gift, what's the next thing that happens?

Well, your first email will be sent out automatically to your lead, so once they put that email in, your autoresponder account will fire off your first welcome email to them along with the free gift! With the technology and software that's available to you, this is very easy to set up.

It isn't required for you to have any coding knowledge or skills to get this done. You can just watch a couple of videos and copy me as I show you how to set everything up. Get this information here on the book bonus page: **www.TonyRichie.com/bookbonus**

Once you do that, you'll successfully have your system up and ready to build an email list, (your email list will be one of your most important assets when building an online business.)

Then in your first email to your subscriber, you would welcome them and tell them a little more about you, plus what they can expect from your free guide and email series following. While in the process of building your email series and funnel, I would build out 5-10 email newsletters that span over 2-4 weeks. Now you know for every lead that you get into the funnel, you'll be automatically communicating with them by email, with your system sending emails on your behalf. What a beautiful thing.

Every market has a different threshold of how many emails you should send, so you'll just have to test it out. I used to send an email out a day to my automotive list, and a lot of them used to reply and say, "too many emails, too many!" So I started cutting them down, and now I'm at about three emails a week, and nobody's complaining.

You can also (through your autoresponder) put a link in the emails to move them to a weekly summary email, instead of all the daily ones, which your autoresponder segregates to a different list. It sounds a lot more complicated than it is, and the great thing about an autoresponder is, it's 'set it and forget it', once you've got everything loaded up.

It's 'set it and forget it', and the other great thing about the autoresponder is once you start building a list, and you have 5,000, 10,000 people on it. Every time you have some sort of new and exciting news coming up you could do a broadcast and send a letter out to everybody in real time. So, if you're doing a sale on your product, or you've got a new blog post or a new video, you can instantly queue up a brand-new email and send it out to your entire database so they can watch the new presentation or check out your sale.

With autoresponder content, you want to remember the 80/20 rule. So, for every five emails I send out I'll have one that's more toward pushing them to buy my product or a promotion of some sort.

If you do this, you should set yourself up to have an overall happy and healthy subscriber list. If all you do is keep promoting your own product, or just constantly selling to them, you'll lose their trust as somebody who is looking out for them. So keep good content coming to them on a weekly basis. They'll thank you for it.

What I do is I give away a free automotive manual, and I give them a one week boot camp. It's basically seven videos teaching them all kinds of stuff on cars. I send out my seven-video series of awesome content. I'm not asking for the kill. I'm not asking for the sale. It's just, "Check this cool video out. I think you're going to learn a lot! Enjoy." I'll send a new email out every 2-3 days for a seven-video series. Then after that we'll get into different content and it's ongoing, then I'll start linking to my main offer page at the very bottom to show them some of the products that I sell.

Your main offer could be a trial. Your main offer could be the full price. It depends on your market and what you're testing out. My main offer that my leads see immediately right after they put their email in, is a special one-time offer. I hit my fresh leads up with a one-time offer on the thank you page for a special trial to test out my product, and in the first email. I give them their free manual. I tell them about the seven-day series.

I tell them about the newsletter, and then I have a little reminder, "PS. This special offer is going to be expiring in the next couple of days." Right now, with my funnel, I sell them right away, but no one says you *have* to do it that way. Just like the old saying goes, there are many ways to skin a cat.

Then I go into the educational email series and don't send them another offer for at least 2 weeks. I'll show them the full price of some of my products. Some will buy. If they don't buy, then you can do your monthly sale, and then people jump on that, because they see the value.

It's always good to have a video sales letter to sell your products, a video presentation that explains what the problem is in the market and how you're about to solve that and make life much easier for them if they buy your product.

The other thing you want to have is this in text format below your video. You know, you have people who are visual, people who like to read, so that's why I have my whole sales letter in, you guessed it, text. And I know in some of the markets I'm involved in, I have a lot of older subscribers, 50-60-year-old guys and they like to read. So, having the dual video and the text bullets and graphics of what they're getting works in combination for my offer pretty good. I'm sure for a lot of other products out there, also. People like to have both, I think. This is important when you get to the point where you are creating the sales material to sell your product. Again, this is not a difficult part; there are some programs and templates that you can use that make the process fairly easy to get done. I also give you more than enough ideas and samples in my trainings if you decide to get into my TC System.

Keep in mind that whenever you're doing the sales video, it takes very little work and costs almost nothing to have someone transcribe it for you, so that way you can offer both modalities.

With this sales process, some of your visitors will immediately purchase your product, and once they do that, you have your autoresponder set up to put them in a customer file rather than a prospect one.

You'll get a lot of people who will never buy. Then you'll get guys who will buy after a year. There's all kinds of people on your list. There's impulsive buyers, people who see your stuff, and they'll want to buy it right away. I've had people go through my free blogs and just write me a testimonial, "Hey, Tony, I never invested in your program, but I was able to complete my whole project just with your free information. Thank you so much!"

Then you'll get the people who buy everything you have to offer. You need to remember what I'm going to tell you right now. People LOVE to buy things. People will always buy stuff. So rather than thinking, "why would they buy my stuff," create your site, your sales funnel and sell! You will make sales if you have something up and running that people can see. If you have nothing up, no fishing nets up and casted out, you will never catch any fish. Let's get it done!

After people go through the seven-day video course, I'll hit them up with 2-3 emails a week with continuing content, news, tips and tricks on this and that, and this is all automated.

Then after about a month or so, I'll do a sale, which is half price for some of my top products for a few days with a deadline. I'll give them a coupon code, or sometimes I'll even just discount it, so when they get to the order page they could just order.

It's an email series that talks about the special, and we have a little sexy countdown timer at the top of the website, so they see that it's real, and it's really counting down, which adds scarcity and makes people want to buy. A lot of people end up jumping on that, because they missed out on the first offer. We built up the value. They see that the course is worth a few hundred bucks, and now we're giving it to them at 50% off for a few days.

We end up selling a lot of people who were on the fence. They take advantage of the offer, and they buy. After sales like this, we also get a lot of emails of people saying, "Hey Tony! I missed out on the sale... I was on vacation. How can I get it? Can you please extend the offer to me?" For people who are honest like that, we say, here's a link, and we'll just email them an order link on the side. My customer support girls will help them place the order.

Then after a sale, we still have those people on our list and you will, too, because they won't just magically disappear. And on a side note, make sure you back up your email list every few months, just in case. This means that you would want to export a copy of your email subscribers just in case you end up with an autoresponder account issue. So, we keep feeding them cool email news and content. Maybe next year they'll buy. Maybe in six months they'll buy. You just want to consistently build your audience and build your list.

Sometimes we even send them information on a different product that we think they'll be interested in. This is called affiliate marketing, where you would offer and sell other people's products and get paid a commission off every sale you made. And with the tracking and systems that are available today, tracking and making sure you get paid for the sale is a breeze. For this I will recommend a site that I use at times called ClickBank.com. We have another product on ClickBank that we offer every once in a while. It's not in the autoresponder, but every few months I'll do a broadcast promoting that, if people haven't jumped on my program.

You can make up to 50% on the sale of someone else's product. The best part - you didn't even have to create it. A lot of people get started online this way, selling other people's products and getting paid a commission. You can build a blog/website and get enough traffic from YouTube and get paid 50%, even before you even create your product. It's a pretty cool way to get started as well.

This also gives you an opportunity to increase your income because there will be those people on your list that will never buy your product, so why not offer something that's similar?

Full disclosure: When I send out a special sale offer and email it to my 50,000-member email list, on average I could earn an additional 5 figures in three to five days.

That's why having a long-term funnel is so critical. It's easy money. And your list is your asset. Take care of them and there is a special way of doing this.

The funnels that I do, I noticed, work better when they're actually live. I tested automated sales through emails, but I notice if I actually record a selfie video and say, "It's Father's Day. I want to do a special Father's Day sale" and have a live video that I actually made that month, I'll get much better results because people see that it's real. If you set up a special sale offer, it's going to take you a half day's work...max. Isn't it worth putting in a half days' work in to get a five-figure payday? Heck yes! Once I discovered how to run and set up these pretty much automated sales campaigns, I did one for every month. Next think I know, I added an extra six figures annually to my business without investing any money in advertising. How cool is that!?!

Then once the people buy my main digital courses, the online membership sites, downloadable book, etc., (about 25% of them like physical books), I offer them a big box of DVDs and books of everything they just got, but it has a little bit more content in it. One of my add-on products is a 22 DVD kit, including four manuals. This is called an up-sell, where you would offer another product immediately after your customer just made a purchase from you. It's a great profit center and if your offer is priced right and a no-brainer, you'll automatically make more sales which, of course, turns into more profit for you.

Hands Off!

The best part is that I don't touch any of the products and you don't have to either! How do we do this? I use a fulfillment center. When somebody buys my hard copy product, my fulfillment company will get an email (from my shopping cart) saying this person bought, please ship to this address, and they'll just ship it right out and send me a confirmation email. It's really hands off. I don't touch any product.

It's every bit as hands off as my digital products are once it's created and properly set up.

I believe you can and should create a business how you want it to work. I didn't want to deal with any physical inventory and shipping out boxes. It was also cost effective for me. It made sense, and there are a lot of legitimate companies that will do that for you. That's their business, to fulfill your products. It's very easy to get set up with great companies.

One of the physical products we sell are spray guns for my automotive business. I partnered with a wholesaler and struck an exclusive deal. They manufacture their guns in Taiwan, and they have their own warehouse in California, and he actually found me a few years ago on YouTube. He asked, "Can you do a review on our spray guns?" She sent me some spray guns to review and I liked them so much I said, "Let's work a deal. I'll sell these for you. What are we looking at?" Side note: I used to be on Amazon with spray guns.

When I first started out I didn't have my own spray guns to sell, so I decided to just be an Amazon partner. On Amazon, I'd sell $150.00 - $300.00 spray guns, and they'd only give you 5% commission, which is peanuts, and in total I'd only earn about $200.00 a month with Amazon commissions. Once I struck my own spray gun deal, it took off. So, let's continue with the story... First, she gave me some spray guns to review. I checked them out and loved the quality and performance so much, I just became a big promoter. I started talking, doing reviews on every gun they had, and I started telling everybody, my entire audience, "hey guys! this is what we use at the headquarters. This is what we use to do our jobs. This is what we used to teach in the course. It's an awesome gun, and we have them for sale in our own store."

Now for every $200.00 spray gun that I sell, I can expect a 25% profit which is a nice margin. He also drop-ships for me. All I do sell them on my site through my shopping cart. At the end of each day my virtual assistant (VA) makes sure they got the orders. This alone has added a few thousand dollars a month in profit to my bottom line. Just by selling spray guns at a better margin. Now instead of a 5% commission from Amazon, we're making at least 25%. Big difference when you make little changes like this. Yes, it does take a little work, but it's worth it.

I would recommend that you never promote something just for the money. Only promote things that are really good for your audience, because in the long term it'll come back to you in ways you just can't imagine. You're the educator and the advocate, so you need to be true to your tribe.

Split Testing Your Website and Offers…

As far as your website funnel and maintenance goes, split testing is one of the most important things that you should do when running your internet business. With some of the software nowadays, it's easy to set up A/B split testing on your pages to see what converts at a higher rate. If one variation doesn't convert better, just swap it for the control, your original page, and start over. This is how you learn and see what works and what doesn't. And the strange thing is, what works this year may not work next year, so it's important to learn this so you know where things are going.

When I say these things, I mean what the market wants, what they're willing to pay, what gets them to respond, prices, etc. Listen, you're probably thinking right now, …. "Tony! This is complicated, man. What the heck are you talking about?" "What! I need to know all of this just to make money online?" The answer is YES. You do need to know the basics and hey, I will tell you that I didn't know squat when I first started my online business.

I will say that most of it is the lingo. The vocabulary. Once you get the basic vocabulary of your online business and understand it, it becomes a hell of a lot easier. It took me a few months of listening to people in the industry through DVD's, courses and seminars that I attended until I started getting it. But I did get it and you can, too. Please remember that I am nobody special. I literally got all D's and F grades in high school - besides gym class. Then I dropped out. If I can get this going and crank out a million-dollar business, I am positive that you can, too! You don't need to be smart to win in this game. You need to be willing to learn the basics and just put them into action and not give up. That's really it. People just give up too easily in life. They take whatever is thrown at them, rather than take responsibility for each and every choice they make. Because whether you like it or not, I will tell you this: You put yourself in the position that you are in right now. You did. If you want a better life, a better future, more happiness, more love, more money, you better start giving now. And as the saying goes, the more you give the more you get. Give love to receive love, spend money to make money. The world shall turn. Invest in yourself to become a better person. Invest in assets, not liabilities. You, yourself can choose to look at yourself as an asset or a liability. Because you're reading this book right now and reading these words I will tell you that you did invest in yourself. You do look at yourself as an asset. Congratulations for that. Now what do I recommend after you finish this book? I say invest further and take yourself to a whole new level. Are you ready, because I will help you get there through one of my intensive training programs called TCS. I will talk more about that at the end of this book and make you a special offer that you can't refuse. But only if you act fast. I am not sure how long I will be doing these special trainings. Anyway, let's get back into the nitty gritty, shall we?

Once you start to track and optimize your funnels, things get really fun. This is how I learned how to lower my customer acquisition cost. You'll get more leads in for less money. I like to start A/B split testing at the very beginning of your funnel, which is your free bribe. You have all these videos on YouTube, you have people clicking the links to get your free stuff. What I constantly do every day is to look at my conversion in the morning, and I'm constantly testing out different pages to see how I can beat my control. I'm always changing headlines, changing button colors, changing text, changing the background color, and it's super easy to do. It only takes a few minutes to make a change, and you reset your stats, and you let it go for another couple of days, and then you see how it's all converting, versus your control.

You constantly optimize. You could have your control converting at 50% for an opt-in. That means for every 100 people that see that page, you're getting 50 leads. 50 people taking action on your page. Then you can simply make a clone of that page, which becomes your A/B split test. You can say ...let me try changing my background to gray instead of black, and just reset it and see what happens. You might get a 47% conversion, so you know the black is still converting better. So you keep that. Maybe you say, I'll change the button color. Instead of green, let's make it orange. Then you test that. It does take time, obviously, but the more traffic you get, the quicker you can get your testing data and results. If you're only getting 10 visitors a day to your site it might take you two weeks to get an idea of what's converting better, but if you're getting a couple hundred people a day, within two, or three days you can figure out which version is doing better for you.

Obviously, the #1 thing is you want to test your opt-in, because that's how many people you're getting into your funnel every day.

Once people go to your funnel you can test out different price points of what you're selling at - free trials, a dollar trial versus a $4.95 trial. There can be many things to test, but I don't stress on it too much when getting started.

The main thing is to just get one offer up. When I say offer, I mean something up and running - your site up and running with a product that you are offering to your visitor to purchase.

If you have one offer up and you're getting visitors, somebody will buy your product. On an average, you should expect a 20-30% opt-in conversion rate. I used to average a 40% conversion on some of my offers, but I finally got it up to the high fifties; one of them is at a 54% conversion, which equates to my income going up. Not bad.

That's why when you have a good control, make sure you don't kill the goose that's laying golden eggs. I'm afraid to say this but I did kill my golden egg layer in the beginning. When I started split testing a few years ago, they didn't have the software that they do now. I had something working, and I changed it out with something, and I totally forgot what was working. I ended up shooting myself in the foot, because I didn't remember. I didn't take a screenshot of the page or what it looked like to remember what was working. So, it's important to at least know what your control is before you start changing things.

That's it for tracking.

Take a deep breath and exhale... come on, it's not that bad. You're reading a book. Give it a little time to soak in. This is all easier to implement than to talk about because you can only do one part at a time. We just did a brain dump on the whole process so don't beat yourself up if you feel a little tired. Maybe you should take a break now... go ahead, take a break, come back later and let's continue because this is about to get even better. I am going to expose some cool YouTube hacks that you can use to make a fortune with your new online business!

Chapter 9

The High Production Myth: Starting with What You Have and Turning It into Your First Million!

Some people use a professional $300 stand to hold a video camera, some people write a full-blown script, some use a story board and others make a huge video production for a 5-minute video. And yes, it may be necessary at times for the right purpose.

But 90% of the time, that's not what I do. That's not what the people who read this book should do. Well, let me put it this way... You don't need any fancy equipment or extensive knowledge to get into this.

We're talking about creating a simple YouTube video. I got started with a $99 Kodak Zi8 HD video camera with manual macro zoom. What does manual zoom mean? It means that I needed to manually move a sliding switch on my camera to clear in on the video if I wanted to get a close-up on a shot. And yes, it's the same video camera that I used to create my first online product, my membership site and all of my YouTube videos. With that camera, I started a 6-figure business in my first 12 months. By month 23 I had nearly made a half million dollars from my videos on YouTube. Because I setup my YouTube channel correctly, YouTube sent targeted traffic to my website which in turn got me tens of thousands of leads with my system selling those leads for me, automatically 24/7. It's a crazy and beautiful thing once you set one of these up for yourself. It's one of the best feelings in the world.

Now, let's talk about what you need to do to get this working for you. However, you must remember that you are at a time in history where something like this is even possible. The timing could never be better.

The trends for video and video marketing are only getting bigger. Start now and get in the game.

So, what do you do before you turn on the camera, or your phone? And talking about phones, yes you probably right now have a better camera and video camera in your pocket (your phone) than when I first started. So yes, you can use your phone and start a business! How cool is that?!?

First, know should have a good idea of who your audience is. In my case, my YouTube subscribers are always commenting on my videos, asking me questions and talking to each other and this gives me great insight about who they are. They tell me what questions that have, their frustrations, what they like and everything in between. Pretty cool!

What I usually do is answer their questions and make a video about it. I take out my iPhone, hit record and start talking and answering their questions. Sometimes I show a sample (about our topic) in the shop or wherever I am. I make it fun and exciting for them.

You can use your arm and hold the phone or even use a selfie stick. I know from personal experience that selfie stick style home-made videos are more down to earth. They don't look like some polished technical thing; even professionals are using them a lot more. Walking around with the camera makes someone look real. It makes you look like you're the one that really did it; that you didn't have the whole staff doing this stuff for you. People are buying information that is easy to find right now, but they're buying the right information sorted out by professionals.

Yes, you could do the selfie, and it's an advantage if you have a friend or someone who can take the film for you to give your audience a different point of view. Just a few days ago, I had my wife grab the camera from me, and she started following me around and filmed me. At times, I have my 8-year-old daughter get in my videos as well. When you think about it, people love it when you start to include a story in your marketing and if you feel comfortable like I do, why not share some of your family members. People love family. It's not like you need to hire a 50-dollar an hour video guy hanging around you just to make a video.

As I write this chapter from Japan — on one of my long-extended trips, I am taking advantage of being in a different location and I always do. You should, too. It's cool to film on my subject matter from a different world point of view, like walking down streets in Japan and showing the difference in cars, the culture, and the foods. People love to live vicariously through you, through your world, and it is a totally different experience for them to enjoy. This is also a great opportunity to build a stronger relationship with your audience.

So, if you're reading this right now and you plan on traveling, take advantage of it and try to think ahead and document the situation.

Again, people are vicarious. They want to live in your lifestyle because they don't see those things normally. That's the reason why they're watching your videos. Keep it engaging; it's a different experience for them. Go to a different location; you never have to always be in the same house or the same garage. Shoot videos while in your car; you could be at the park or at the beach, making videos of anything interesting and most of all talking about what you are an expert in. Making videos while you're out and about is another great tip.

Obviously when in your car, you can't hold the selfie stick, but there's a special mount that you can buy and mount it right in the dashboard or to your windshield, so you can talk and drive at the same time. In fact, it's absolutely easy and you can get one for less than $20. For your reference, I am giving you all of the links and resources, so check them out at **www.TonyRichie.com/bookbonus.**

I previously mentioned about using questions from my audience to create new content. When I first got started, I employed tricks to speed up my knowledge on my audience, because knowing your audience really matters. Since I, too, am really my own audience, I just thought about the most common things people wanted to hear about, and I did research on YouTube, typing in keywords that I am interested in, and I saw the videos and I said, "Ohhh, okay, they're getting a pretty good amount of views. I could talk about the same thing but from a different angle." I also searched in Google. I just typed in the search keywords for my topic and started researching, seeing what people were talking about, reading forums and discovering what the searchers in my market were really looking for. Seeing what problems they were talking about so I could go out and answer them. At times, you'll have to step up your own game and do the research for these questions, but in doing so, you'll become even more knowledgeable and able to share it at a more natural tone.

You might have to read more books on your subject. You want to make sure you are an expert on that; you want people to think you're an expert. So you learn to be the expert. I once heard a few marketers out there say, "You just need to know a little bit more than the person who is buying your product" And I get it. It does make sense and it is true because that's exactly what I did. But as time went on, I started to learn more about what I was sharing and teaching so I could go on and educate others even more. It's really easy. It's the learn and teach society. This is the way the world turns now, and it's amazing because you can literally build an audience and make money by doing this in such a short amount of time. But there is a trick to make this work. You need to know the formula, wrap your mind around it, believe it, and understand the game.

You must first understand that everything in this world revolves around the decimal point. It's ok to be creative, talented and knowledgeable, but if you don't know how to turn that into money for yourself and your family, what is the use? You need to learn how to become artistic, creative, knowledgeable and commercial at the same time. I know that some of you are saying "Tony, I am not a salesman. I can't sell." But the reality is, selling happens every day and whether you know it or not, you are selling every single day. I can write about selling and marketing all day and that's not the purpose of this book. I will save that for another book. The deal is that if you want to have total control of your life, all you need to do is have some knowledge of product creation, understand that marketing is key, and learn how to see effectively. And you don't need to sell like the olden days, that's the cool thing about being online. You set your selling systems up once, and it will sell for you automatically 24/7/365. By learning how to use YouTube and video with me, you'll be on your way to a video marketing ninja.

If you pick a book on photography or real estate, for example, and it has 10 chapters in it, those are already 10 videos that you can make. Just twist up the words and make good videos out of them. You'll just say it from your point of view. You never plagiarize anybody; you just take a common idea on the niche and give your point of view. Creating content is easy. I also subscribe to a lot of blogs or other industry leaders just to see what's working and what's not.

Rightfully so, every person learns from another person. There's no such thing as original content nowadays. We're getting ideas from it; it's just an evolving thing. The only content that was original was the alphabet. And everything that happens then was just a rearrangement of the alphabet.

Tips for Shooting Your Videos

Now, let's talk about tips and things to avoid while shooting the videos. For instance, don't wear sunglasses unless it's part of your character, but

I think it would be harder to pull off in a serious market. Sounds crazy, but you'd be surprised how many make this mistake. People want to see your eyes. A lot can be said with just one look. People can't trust you if they can't fully see you.

One important thing about videos, and this is a fact, is that people would rather have quality audio and forgive you for bad video. If you have a video, people will like it more if the audio is clear because they can hear you well, rather than having a super clear video but with poor audio quality. What's helpful is to invest in at least a lapel mic or a little mic for your camera to get good audio. When I first started out, I didn't have any of that. I was only using the regular camera mic and then probably about a year after, I wised up a little; I invested in a mic and the audio was much better, especially for my paid member content. How did I know this? Because in my members' area people were saying "Ooh, the audio is not that great Tony." I started fixing the issues and it was a lot better for my members. Another tip is to always listen to customer feedback and if it makes sense to you, do what it takes to make things and the quality of our course, and delivery better. It's a good long term strategy because as you start to grow and sell more products, you'll just have happy and satisfied customers. So, if you can, learn from my mistake and Invest in a little mic if possible. They have these little ones now that you could hook right up into your iPhone. They can be also hooked on your shirt collar. No matter which way you turn when you're doing something active, like working in the field or doing a demo, your audio quality will remain crisp and clear.

That's very important because people nowadays are listening with headphones a lot of the time, so they don't want to hear something real loud or something real quiet. It subconsciously turns them off what would otherwise make great content.

Some of these nasty background noises are blowing in the background or wind in the mic. That's horrible, and I'm embarrassed to say that some of my videos in the beginning were like that. You could hardly hear what I'm saying. Better to avoid that from the beginning.

Framing Your Video

Next thing is how to frame when you're getting ready to shoot a video. You start by shooting a little test video to see what the camera is going to see before you spend 7 or 8 minutes going through your whole pitch and then find out there's something in the camera's view that you don't want to be seen; for example, your home address, among others if you're shooting in front of your house. If you're shooting with your selfie stick, just make sure and be aware of your background. There are things you may not want to be seen.

The same goes when using your camera on a tripod, or when doing a green screen in your office to make sure the framing is set correctly, so you don't have anything in the background that you don't want to be seen.

Make sure you know how the lighting is. It's important to test out the lighting before you get into a full-length video, along with your audio. I've made videos where I thought my mic was on, but it was not! One time, I recorded a 20-minute training video on a whiteboard and didn't know the audio was off. I later had to reshoot the whole thing! And it happened a few times. It still happens to the best of us. So always do a test run. Make sure your mic is on and plugged in correctly to your camera and that the lighting is good. You may need to move your lighting around a few times. Home lighting kits, office lighting kits and green screens are all available in the market, but you don't need to go crazy with that. I bought my home setup, a green screen with three camera lights, for about a hundred and fifty dollars off Amazon. It's very inexpensive to set up an in-home recording studio nowadays.

Editing Your Videos

Alright, now that we're framed and were ready to start shooting, do you have to get it right all the way through? No. We don't have to get the video right all the way through especially if you made a mistake in the middle of the video. You can just say, "Cut," pause for 3 or 4 seconds, and then restart from before the mistake, and you can tie those together during your editing process. You don't have to do 7 minutes without taking a breath, but if you can, then great! But there may be times you'll just want to do it again. You could probably come off better the second time around; it all depends. This is how I like to look at it when I do a video and realize that my mic was off - I try to stay positive and just do it again! Ha-ha.

If you do make a mistake while talking in your video, putting that pause in makes it easy during the editing process. You can split it where the audio goes down and pick it back up. It makes editing a lot easier.

Now, we are shooting the video, the lighting is good, the audio pretty much done, and we don't have to say everything correctly. If you're recording your training session for your membership site, I recommend doing a whole bunch of them within a day. In my case I would map out, for example, Chapters 1, 2, and 3, and make one full day a recording day and just try to bang all of them out. I usually like to do them in chunks like that. Bang them all out, and then the next day, just do your editing and the course is pretty much done. If you think you don't want to learn simple video editing, you could hire somebody, but I say especially in the beginning, learn it. It's really not hard and if I can do it, you can.

A lot of beginners who were starting to make their first product thought that they had to do long training videos with a lot of content. Now they've learned that short little videos about one specific thing are much easier. People can go right to what it is that they need, and more than that, it gives you multiple videos to display in your membership site. So instead of doing one 20-minute video, you might have four 5-minute videos. It looks like you have a lot more content in the membership area, plus it really saves the person time if they have to listen to a 20-minute video just to get the one thing that they're looking for. But again, at times with certain training formats, you may need to do a longer 15-20-minute video to make sure your customer/student gets the idea. I use both styles in my courses.

And you could edit this up. It pumps up the volume of what's inside the course and will be easier to navigate for them. So it's a win-win, plus it's really easy to do a 3-5 minute video right the first time than it is to do a 20-minute video. It saves a lot of editing time as well.

iMovie (for mac) and Camtasia (for Windows and Mac) are simple editing softwares that I use and teach in my main course.

Rather than hiring somebody for 30 dollars an hour to do it, you can do it yourself once you master this pretty simple software. It wasn't until 7 years in that I hired my first video guy.

If you have a really good video and the sound for one reason or the other bounces around, you can flatten out the sound, or compress it; your editing software will compress the audio so that it stays smooth. This means that in your editing software there's a little gauge that shows your audio quality. Just like you have in stereos, as the audio is played, the light is bouncing up and down. You have to make sure that by compressing it, nothing goes into the red area. The software automatically does that, and it's one of the reasons why you run your video through the software, even if it doesn't need any editing. Just a reminder… in uploading, be sure to use the checklist to make certain that you upload the video not just in YouTube, but also in your backup sources. Protect your assets. These become valuable as they grow.

Again, with YouTube, get your keywords right, get your tags right, make sure there's a catchy headline, a nice description, and a transcript of the video to add into your description box. Always make sure your URL weblink is above the fold so people can click it easily and don't forget your eye-catching thumbnail image. I show you how to apply all of this in greater detail through my videos inside of the TCS program so be sure to check that out after reading this book.

Furthermore, make sure that your outro incorporates a "Call to Action" and in the chapter above that is what we previously discussed. YouTube doesn't have any problems with you selling and advertising your products. They gauge all their videos on watch time, so even if you are selling in our video, and people are sticking around to watch it, you'll do great and you'll get more and more views.

Here's a really good tip to help get your videos watched for the longest amount of time...

It's a proven fact that shorter videos perform better on YouTube. 4 minutes and 20 seconds to be exact. It's the perfect-length video.

If you're putting out content and you want people to watch most of your videos and you've got an engaging 4-min video, you're off to a great start. Once you start building a subscriber base, and you have people liking your channel and subscribing, then I would move your strategy to a longer 8- to 12-minute video. Because from what I am seeing, and by talking to account managers on YouTube as well as other consultants, this is where it's moving.

I wouldn't do 30- to 40-minute videos. I see a lot of people doing them, but I don't think it's a good starting out strategy.

I've also noticed some YouTubers mentioning how long their video is in the beginning. This way, the person knows that it's only a 4-minute video, and they have time to watch it rather than to make them guess how long the video is going to be. Of course, YouTube posts the length of the video, so people know before they click, and that's something I do in my broadcast.

So, if I have a quick little 6-minute tutorial on something, I'll say, "Hey, watch this 6-minute video on 'this and that'." It gives them a timeframe, which is a good thing to do.

For instance, one of my popular videos is on how to paint a car in 12 minutes. It's a 12-minute video, longer than I wanted to do, but it ended up being great and right now it's close to 800,000 views in 8 months, which is a lot of targeted views. People will watch a longer video if it's really captivating and engaging. But that's not the rule.

Live videos such as YouTube Live or Facebook Live

Something fairly new are live video feeds that you can host on Facebook and on YouTube. These are really great to play with, and if the video doesn't turn out the way you wanted it to be, you can always delete it. Playing with live video will build up your skills on being in front of the camera live.

I've done around 20 live stream videos so far, and with YouTube live, I've noticed that each time that I do one, I get more and more people joining in. When I first started out I had around 30 people on it. Then, it turned into 55, then 70 and recently I had 150 people live watching one of my YouTube live streams. It was cool because you get to interact live with your audience and get to know them.

It's also good to inform them ahead of time when you'll be live. I would even say a day ahead of your scheduled live video and then send a follow-up email an hour before you go live. It will increase your attendees dramatically. The thing with that is once you go live on YouTube, it takes a good 5 to 10 minutes for people to start joining in. And remember, if you're doing live streams with YouTube or Facebook, they're going to be longer. The video show that you host will not be a 5-10-minute clip. You'll want to stay on longer because it does take time for people to tune in and the longer you stay on, you'll notice more and more people keep tuning in.

So think of a topic that you can talk about for at least 15-20 minutes. I say this because I start my YouTube lives with one main topic that I want to talk about and I'll talk about that main piece of content for about 10-15 minutes. I give them a good jam packed 10-15 minutes of useable content that they like, then I open it up for live Q&A. People seem to love this, so I keep doing it and my sales have been going up by doing this because I talk about and promote my paid programs while doing these shows.

Another thing, when I started doing my YouTube live, I treated it like a Webinar. I started to make it very engaging, like I would raise my hand. Of course, they would see me on my computer camera. I was like "Are you liking this so far? Type in the chat." I would always encourage them to type in the chat. Then, I would start off with "Hey, where are you from? Type in where are you from. Ohhh, we got somebody in Atlanta. Ohhh, we got somebody in Florida. We got Australia in the house." That would make the video very engaging. I would go on and say "The more you give me, the more I can give you" So I treat it like a real training call, and the engagement goes up like crazy, and people stick around. A hundred and fifty live people on my last one. It was fun. Remember that it is a visual and auditory audience. If you have some little things to hold up while you're talking and answer questions about that thing you're holding up, people will like that.

Tube Cash

When I was in Japan, I was like "Guys, wanna see where I'm at in Japan? You wanna see the rooms, the apartment where I'm staying in?" You're going to look outside, and people in the chat would type "yeah, yeah I wanna see!" so I'll just grab my laptop, walk out around the house, and show them outside, and they're loving it.

Tube Cash

Chapter 10

Ready, Aim, Fire: Want the Good Life?
Just Get Started!

When it all comes down to it, just start up a YouTube channel on what you like to talk about and what you're knowledgeable in. We see people out there in dog training, fitness, coaching, sports, food and drink, travel, finance, math and even in automotive repair. I started off talking about things relating to cars and helping people get good car deals. I get people from the USA, Australia, New Zealand and Asia going to my website and asking me questions about cars. You could start with anything that you have, and it doesn't have to be just about your passion. It could even be something that you want to get into and now is the best time to start.

They say the best way to learn something is to teach it. So, if you have something that you're curious about, even if you don't know much about it, start learning about it and teaching it back to others. Because as you teach it, you're going to do more research and learn more about it anyway. And once you start building an audience, you'll have more communication with them, they'll start asking you questions and if you don't know the answers, you do a bit more research and you could educate yourself and you can continue to educate them. Pretty cool if you ask me.

It's basically like passing on information through an information river. As long as you set up your funnels and your website correctly, you could turn it into a profitable business for yourself. I don't know if the silkworm farming market is going to be profitable and a good one to get in because something like that is so niched out and small. You have to make sure whatever you're getting into is profitable, right?

So after you figure something out, go online and do a little bit of keyword research and see if you have enough people searching for that topic. And if it looks like enough people are searching it, and there's a problem people want to solve, then it may be worth creating a product. I'd start asking them questions to see what they want. And if you get enough of that, then you build out a little mini product and you start selling it online.

Once you narrow in where you want to get started, the next step is to do some keyword and market research to see what's out there on the internet. Go to Google and type in, just for example, "dog training." We're going to say "How to train your German shepherd." We're going to check out all the blogs, we're going to see how many blogs there are and we'll show you how to use Alexa, a tool that shows how much traffic/visitors a site is getting. And if it looks like it's getting a lot of traffic and you see that people are selling products like dog care products or information products in the dog market, then you know it's profitable. That's a great sign that people are buying things in that market. People are passionate about it. They have a lot of questions, and it's a thriving market.

Doing your market and keyword research is probably one of the most important parts that you must hone in on when getting started. Go to the Google keyword tool, and you actually have to create a free AdWords account to get access to the keyword research tool. I'll show you exactly how to do this as well. So, you just create a basic Google account like we talked about earlier in this book. But again, if you're getting into an already thriving market, there is no need to get into the nitty-gritty keyword research from the start. It's more important that you think of your USP and your hook at that point to see how you'll end up entering the market to compete and dominate your space.

Here's how basic keyword research is done. You get a Gmail/Google account and then you create your AdWords account, which is free by the way. And you type in the keyword tool "how to train a German shepherd" Once you put that keyword in, it'll show you the monthly estimated search within Google. As an example, it will give you an estimate that people are searching for that keyword 500,000 times a month on Google. You'll be able to instantly see how big or small a market is. And you know if it's a market that you can jump right in and compete.

Honestly, I don't look at other people in the same space as me as competitors. I look at them to learn from, to get ideas from, and possibly to start a partnership with if they are willing to. The best way to introduce yourself into a market is to offer something that your competitors don't offer. Go the extra mile and stand out and make a statement. Now, when you're doing keyword research, and you end up with a very low search volume niche like silkworm farming and you find out there are only 25 searches a month for it, you know that you should probably be doing something else. It's not a very big market and you're basically wasting your time. Move on to something that gets more searches in the world.

It's important to know your market before jumping in and to have an idea of how many people are searching for what you'll be offering. And honestly, if you find a keyword that has at least 8,000 to 50,000 searches a month, depending on the market, it's a pretty good start. You can easily build a website business that makes a couple of thousand dollars a month with that kind of search volume. Plus, if you see other people selling products, then you know for a fact that you can jump in and compete pretty easily.

Once you've decided and are ready to get into your market, you'll want to put up your lead capture page. Remember, we talked about this earlier in the book - get a little squeeze page up saying, "FREE Report Reveals 3 Unknown and Easy Steps To Potty Train Your German

Shepherd in 2 Days or Less!" People will then put their email in and you send them three little steps that you promised them.

In your follow-up email, instantly you could say "Hey, what's the most burning question that you have about training your dog?"

Not everybody's going to fill out the forms and give you all the information, but you'll get a group of people who will and you'll start to build an avatar of exactly what kind of person is interested in your products and in your website. Once you get that, you'll cultivate that information from all these people, build an avatar and start learning how to speak their language.

Once you start speaking to people in their own language, it becomes easier to sell them things. Example, in the automotive market people will say certain keywords. They'll know tool brand names or certain abbreviations that you could use in your talk. It just makes them feel more comfortable with you even if they're reading your email or if they're listening to an audio from you. It just makes it so much easier to sell, so it's very important to learn who your audience is. It's basically proof showing them that you are just like them. People want to feel connected to you before they give you money.

With Google analytics (which you will have installed on your site), you're going to see a lot more demographics on what kind of people are visiting your website. What age range, what countries they're coming from, what states they're coming from. It can get really technical once you get into it, but you don't have to start at a techie level. It doesn't have to be like that. The first step is to actually start a dialogue. Just start talking and emailing a couple of people to get to know them. That's how you start building out an avatar of your ideal customer.

When I got started years back in my automotive niche, a lot of my old followers used to be pretty much across the board when it came to demographics. After I had a couple of hundred customers, I'd started doing some surveys and I would have a specific survey question where it asked their age range. It was always 20% across the board, pretty much even. I had a very broad audience. But I noticed a few years later that it moved to the older guys, the 45 to 65-year-old males who are interested in my stuff. Now, because of this knowledge, I market a little differently than I would to a younger audience.

The age thing can start out across the board, but eventually you do hone in on it. I'm just guessing that these guys had more discretionary income than I originally thought. These weren't poor guys trying to save a buck. These were guys that could afford to buy the tools and that sort of thing, but they just wanted the experience of repairing cars themselves.

With my car sales website, the crowd was more of a business opportunity audience. They want to make some money. But for my auto customization audience, those guys were more of a 'retire with extra income.' They wanted to redo their hot rods themselves and feel the DIY pride of doing their own project instead of just paying a body shop $15,000 and having it done. It's something that these guys wanted to do all their lives but just didn't have any guidance, so they invested in my program.

Becoming the Expert

An easy way to get started, and this is how I did it, is to position yourself as someone of authority. You want to come off like you're the expert and you simply want to help them.

So, by talking about tips and tricks of the topic you automatically position yourself as an expert because not anybody will just start creating and uploading videos to YouTube. Also, when you people offer more free information (your free bribe), this just compounds the effect for you. Offer your free bribe and if you don't have one created yet, simply set up a form that says that you want to help them. Example:

"What is your most burning question about ABC? Fill your name and email and tell me what your most burning questions are and I will reply to you personally with some answers."

You can use this information to create your product and your free bribe. That's how you build up a free report because people are going to be asking you questions and you'll eventually have all of the information that you need to create a killer free report (which would be your free bribe) and even enough information to crank out an amazing product.

You're going to start to recognize the most common questions. Out of fifty responses, you will notice many people will have the same question and you'll know for sure to include it in your free bribe.

Don't think you're a writer? Hire a freelance editor for $50 bucks and get your report polished up. It's really as simple as that. It's relatively inexpensive to do. You could go to a place called elance.com They have writers there. If you're really on a tight budget, you could also hire a Filipino in the Philippines to draft up a report for you. It's very inexpensive, and I say for less than a hundred dollars you can have a 20 to 30-page report done, edited and looking really good. You could even get the graphics for the cover done very easily. I go a lot more in-depth about all of this on video, so if this feels a bit complicated over text format here, be sure to check out **www.TonyRichie.com/bookbonus** to get more information about all of this and how you can really put all of this together pretty easily, and how my team and I can help you. How awesome is that?

Okay, we've covered the first part, getting information by questioning your market to create your free bribe.

Now, create your main product using the same technique. It could be more of an in-depth 50-75-page manual. It could be your main product and then you could make a couple of bonus videos that go with it (this automatically enhances your products value and you can also charge higher prices if you do this.) I can get into a small habit hole about pricing, but let's stick on topic for now. The video part of your course can be you showing them what's already in the paid manual and going over by screen cam and getting more detailed about your course, etc.

Or, you could even talk live right in front of your computer or even better, you illustrate it. Like you go into your training area (let's say you're a dog trainer) and you shoot a live in-the-field video of you training a dog. The more you can appeal to the person's senses, the more valuable the product is going to be to the person.

In my blockbuster trainings, you will find details on how to actually package your products and make it so appealing, your audience will be begging you to buy from you. No joke. I made it really easy for you to copy and get this done for yourself. It's a simple process when you have a guide that shows you how to get things done step-by-step.

You Getting Paid...

Once your lead wants to buy your product, how do they send you money and how do you send them the product?

Right now, it's so easy. There are so many software and shopping carts that you can use, and we recommend a few of the best ones out there that are very easy on the pocket, and easy to setup. First of all, you could easily use PayPal and you can even accept all major credit cards with them. You also have Braintree and Stripe for credit card processors. You can get set up with most merchant accounts within a day. I will admit that Braintree takes a little longer to get accepted, but they're a good company. You'll be able to accept any major credit card from anywhere in the world and start accepting payments from your site and it's pretty simple.

Next, you'll want to build out your mini sales funnel, a mini sales page that shows what you're offering is a great start. You place your button that says "order now." It takes them to the order page where your user will fill out their name, information, email, credit card number and as soon as they hit submit, boom, it'll take them to a thank you page where it'll say "Thank you. Here's how to access your order."

We show you how to create and run simple sales pages and membership sites that deliver your products automatically to your customers. This is stuff that you can do in a day if you have all of the text and content that you want to put on your pages. I would say if you're starting out with nothing and an idea pad, take no more than a week to get your sales system up and running. Isn't it worth a week's work to make automated sales 24/7/365? Yeah, I think so. Even for a non-techie. It's gotten very simple now with all the technology. I'm a non-techie guy, I don't do any coding, and I can do it all so easily. All of the systems that I use are literally drag and drop, fill out blank text boxes, easy.

And if you're a super non-techie guy, there are VA's and freelancers out there that can help you with any area that you may have an issue in. But seriously, if you took just a little time to learn this, I can show you how to set the entire thing up from A-Z step-by-step. And once you get things humming, you can hire VA's for as little as $2.00 an hour in the Philippines to help you manage your sales and support. Everything I teach is point and click. If you can just watch my screen, pause the video, do it exactly as I do, you'll have a working, running website in days. You'll be accepting payments from anybody anywhere in the world. It's just a matter of getting targeted traffic, and you do that by uploading more to YouTube.

That Personal Touch

Let's talk about setting up ongoing customer care and taking care of your leads and customers. Imagine your business is humming and you've got 30 or 40 videos up on YouTube and you're getting a steady stream of traffic coming to your website.

People are putting in their name and email to get your free information, your bribe. They're going through your mini email funnel that automatically builds a relationship and sells your product. And you have your product set up, your order page set up and they're buying your products. It becomes really fun and exciting.

Once you initially get setup you could probably handle the amount of customer service coming in. Obviously once you start making sales and you're making money, you're going to get a percentage of people that want a refund. They say it's not for them or they're having problems logging in or they couldn't get their download link. And in the beginning, you're probably not going to be making 50 sales a day or 30 sales a day to where all you're doing all day is customer support. You can probably do most of it yourself. I was doing all of that myself until I hit $10,000 a month in sales. After that I was like "man, I don't want to do customer service anymore." Because at that point I was probably doing two to three hours of customer service a day. It wasn't hard work, I just didn't want to do that anymore. I knew that my time was better off spent on marketing and making more videos to get more traffic and sales. When you get to this point, you could hire a VA from the Philippines and pay them $1.50 to $2.00 an hour and have them take care of all of your customer support for you. It's inexpensive and affordable to hire help online. Imagine having your own dedicated personal virtual assistant helping you with all of your support issues and more for less than $2.00 US an hour. It's awesome. Now, let's move on to what you do after you launch your product.

It's very important in the beginning to get feedback on your product. It's a brand-new product and some people may have issues with it. They might not like certain sections of it or they're asking questions. You may need to create and add in certain parts to better your course, or to make it easier for them to understand and consume. So, I would recommend to really pay attention to your customers and what their questions are, especially in the beginning. You should answer these questions. It's very important to actually be there, be proactive, see what people are saying, get feedback. It's a great time to start improving your course and tweaking things a little so as your business grows, so you'll have less customer support to deal with. And you'll know the most common questions and you'll have little template emails to reply back to people with. Sometimes people are going to have the same sort of questions and you'll be able to create little templates that you could pass off to your VA.

It's also very important, once you have your whole business on auto pilot and you let it go for six months or a year, that you check your customer support every occasionally, just to see what people are writing in. Yes, your appointed assistant will be handling all of this for you, but it's good to keep the feedback coming to you as well. You could have her send you important emails so you can stay on top of your business.

There was a point in my business where I was so busy and focused on my other sites and creating other products that I missed checking customer support for weeks, but after checking, you're like "oh wow, I need to go fix this or I need to go create another video that'll help people out on this" so they don't ask this questions which will reduce customer support. It's always important to go in every once in a while, just to see what the people are saying because they are buying your products...

You don't want to be completely absent and not know what's going on because everything's always changing. The market's always changing and so it's important to do that.

If it's done right, your customer service team or single VA, will make you money. When you have customers asking for a refund, a lot of times it can simply be that they haven't been able to access the course, or they can't find what they need. And if you get them help quickly, most times you'll be able to save the sale.

A lot of times solving their problem means they need the next step in your program (an advanced program) and they actually end up spending more money rather than getting a refund.

Prospects and leads are wonderful, but people that've already taken their credit card out and given you money are the easiest people to sell more stuff to.

Don't build a company that's a one product deal. Keep evolving, and keep creating products and adding more products to your business. Give people what they want. Keep asking and taking surveys, create new programs and sell more. This is how you can easily grow your business. And don't switch industries just because you get bored. You may switch industries or broaden your niches because it's a sound business decision and makes sense because maybe it would allow you to cross promote your products. Do it for those reasons. Not because you want to get into something totally new. If you do that, you're just starting from scratch again. A good rule and key to success is to build on top of what you already have going.

Don't think just because you were great in one niche, that you can be great in another market without a lot of research. People tend to forget the start-up phase and think "well, I made $10,000 a month doing this, I can make $10,000 a month doing anything." Be quick to fix problems, but be slow to move in to other areas that you are not too familiar with. Broaden your business but don't over-extend yourself and kill the golden goose.

If it's a business that's doing well for you, you want to make sure you have customer support down and you want to make sure your products are great, the feedback continues to be great and you continue to market it. Continue to create videos for it. Don't just let it die out.

Once you have a winning website, a winning product, you will always have to maintain it. Once you have that under control, then go out and test other markets and build another website and get into other areas.

I started in the automotive business because I knew a lot about the automotive world and I created products and sold products in that industry, and by doing that, through the years, I've learned so much about marketing and sales. I now feel like I could teach other people and inspire others to creating their own online businesses. That's why I decided to write this book. What this business has done for my family and I is truly amazing. I am living my dream. Without this book getting out and selling thousands of copies, I will still be fine. I am just so passionate and thankful and so amazed at how anybody, if they want to, could do the same as I've done. I truly want to help others break free from the 9-5 daily grind and help better the world by helping more people live their dreams. I know I can do it, and this is my next mission. This is why I want to get my story out to you. I hope it has inspired to realize that you can do the same.

Getting To The Next Level

Yes, parts of the book may have sounded confusing if you're new to the industry, but it's all right. That's normal. I felt the same when I got started. Remember when I said the hardest part when getting into a new business or field is the vocabulary and the terms? Well, you'll have to go through some of that learning curve and it will take a little bit of time, but not much. Look, if I came from knowing nothing about this industry, not computer literate at all, with no formal education and make $150,000 during my first year online, then hey.. stop making excuses. If you are interested in taking all of this to the next level, I am ready to help you build out your very own TubeCash business. To get my resources and bonuses, plus some free training over video on how this business really looks and operates as if it's your own, then go to **www.TonyRichie.com/bookbonus** and put in your information. I will be looking forward to working with you.

Let's make the next 12 months of your life the best ever. May all of your dreams and desires come true. But remember, to get anything out of life, you must believe, have faith and act at the same time. Take action and meet me here **www.TonyRichie.com/bookbonus.**

Talk soon and see you at the TOP!

-Tony Richie

P.S. - It's because you're constantly developing. You're always learning from other people. Younger people, older people. It's constantly learning and putting what you learn into action. That's what I like to do. I just continue to learn.

As your new business grows, you have the option of doing what I do. Try to automate it as much as possible, then maybe expanding into other niches if you feel that you can execute on it. But you don't just walk away from a business that's making you money - you have an asset. Take care of it because it can be life changing if you take it seriously.

About the Author

"A True, True Marketer," Tony Richie has been living the online dream and traveling the world with his wife and two daughters since 2009.

With his unique videos, Tony has become an internet and YouTube sensation within the automotive and online business niches. Tony knows how video traffic works and how to leverage it to its fullest. Would you like to have video working for you 24/7 automatically driving traffic, collecting hot leads, and making sale for you?

Tony now consults and helps businesses build their own brand channel by using strategic YouTube videos and a custom channel that is optimized to get the job done. As you know, video will make up over 80% of internet search traffic by 2021.

"If you're not using strategic video in your business right now, you're leaving your money and your brand exposure on the table. And the best part is that YouTube is a very business friendly platform, so it's easy to get started."

www.TonyRichie.com
Free Book Bonus Page: www.TonyRichie.com/bookbonus
Tony@TonyRichie.com
Office: 1-800-683-1726

www.ingramcontent.com/pod-product-compliance
Lightning Source LLC
Chambersburg PA
CBHW051718170526
45167CB00002B/710